Jumpstarting Communication Skills in Children with Autism

A PARENTS' GUIDE TO APPLIED VERBAL BEHAVIOR

TOPICS IN AUTISM

Jumpstarting Communication Skills in Children with Autism

A PARENTS' GUIDE TO APPLIED VERBAL BEHAVIOR

Mary Jane Weiss, Ph.D., BCBA-D & Valbona Demiri, Ph.D., BCBA-D

Sandra L. Harris, Ph.D., series editor

Woodbine House ◆ 2011

KH

Published in the United States of America by Woodbine House, Inc.,
6510 Bells Bell Rd., Bethesda, MD 20817. 800-843-7323. www.woodbinehouse.com

Library of Congress Cataloging-in-Publication Data

Weiss, Mary Jane.
Jumpstarting communication skills in children with autism : a parents' guide to applied verbal behavior / by Mary Jane Weiss, Valbona Demiri,. -- 1st ed.
p. cm. -- (Topics in autism)
Includes bibliographical references and index.
ISBN 978-1-890627-70-6
1. Autistic children--Language. 2. Communicative disorders in children. 3. Parents of autistic children. I. Title.
RJ506.A9W43 2011
618.92'85882--dc23

2011021990

Manufactured in the United States of America

First Edition
10 9 8 7 6 5 4 3 2 1

3/6/12

This book is dedicated to our mothers
Joan Rita Coneys and Qamile Kadrijaj Demiri
and to our children
Liam, Nora, Julia, Magnolia,
Eudora, Orion
and to all of the mothers and children we have been privileged to know in our work

Table of Contents

Acknowledgements

Mary Jane thanks colleagues who have inspired her in understanding and applying Verbal Behavior to individuals with autism, especially Mary Barbera, Andy Bondy, Barbara Esch, Mark Sundberg, and Jim Partington. She also thanks her community of colleagues, especially mentor Sandra Harris and collaborator Suzanne Buchanan, and her friends in the Autism SIG and in the Autism NJ community. She deeply thanks the children and adults with autism she has known, and their families, for teaching her about strength and courage. She also thanks her friends (especially Lisa and Ellen) and family (especially Bill, Joan, Danny, and Ilse) for their flexibility, support, encouragement, and inspiration.

Val thanks Christian for his unconditional love, encouragement, and humor. She also thanks the extraordinary colleagues, children, and families in her life who have fostered and cultivated her understanding of autism, ABA, and the joy in productive work. She especially thanks Rita Gordon and Mary Jane for their mentorship and for modeling strength, independence, and empowerment. The longtime support of an amazing EI team consisting of Therese, Jaci, Jacey, Danielle, Agnes, and Lucy is deeply appreciated. A special thank you to dear friends, Jenny and Erin, as well as Ellen and Therese, who have put their hearts in all they do.

We both thank our longtime collaborators at Rutgers University, especially Sandra Harris, Lara Delmolino, Rita Gordon, Bob LaRue, and Marlene Brown. We also both thank the entire Woodbine staff, especially Susan Stokes, whose superb editing was transformative, Beth Binns, and Fran Marinaccio. We also thank each other!

Introduction

In recent years, autism has received increasing attention in the media, from the medical community, and from the community at large. As a result, the visibility of the disorder has increased.

One benefit of this increased exposure in the media is that children are indeed more likely to be identified as having autism. Pediatricians are more likely to note delays and to refer children for full evaluations. Parents are more likely to hear about the possibility of autism when the child is a young toddler. Access to services at young ages is more common than ever. And yet, it can still be confusing for parents to navigate the diagnostic and service challenges.

Although there is evidence that the sooner services are started, the better, often families spend months or even years trying to determine what the optimal treatment for their child might be. In particular, if a young child with autism is not communicating well or at all, parents may feel a real sense of urgency in trying to locate the right services to help their child begin to progress in acquiring speech and language skills. This book has been written to help these families understand and obtain the help their children need.

The Autism Spectrum

Autism disorders are generally agreed to fall along a spectrum, with some children significantly affected, others less so, and still others only mildly affected. Regardless of the degree of impairment, however, autism is described as having three central defining characteristics.

They are:

1. qualitative impairment in reciprocal social interaction;
2. qualitative impairment in verbal and nonverbal communication and in imaginative ability; and
3. markedly restricted and repetitive repertoire of behavior, activities, and interests.

The ways in which these characteristics are manifested are highly variable. While some individuals with autism are not interested in social interaction, others are affectionate and interested in, and attached to, others. While some individuals with autism do not use speech to communicate, others do. When speech is used communicatively, however, the speech often has unusual qualities. Among children with autism spectrum disorders, vocal speech ability frequently lags behind their communication potential. For example, a child may only request wanted items and not be able to hold conversations, or may converse only about topics of special interest.

Some children show restricted behaviors and interests through classically autistic rocking or flapping. Other children may adhere to rituals or routines or fixate on a single object or topic.

It is estimated that about 75 percent of children with autism have developmental delays (APA, 2000). In addition, their development tends to be uneven or scattered, with clear strengths and weaknesses evident. Behavioral difficulties are common, occurring in about 90 percent of individuals with autism. At least 10 to 20 percent of people with autism exhibit severe behaviors such as aggression and self-injury (Lovaas, 1987; Smith, McAdam, & Napolitano, 2007).

Who Is This Book For?

This book will focus primarily on recognizing and improving impairments in verbal and nonverbal communication in young children with ASD ages approximately fifteen months to ten years old. Because communication skills are inextricably linked with social skills, there will also be some discussion of problems with social interaction and how to improve these skills.

Although the book will cover communication issues for children all along the autism spectrum, it will focus more on issues that affect children who are moderately or significantly affected by autism, since these are the children who are most likely to be diagnosed with autism at a young age.

Most young children who are diagnosed at an early age receive either the diagnosis of autistic disorder or pervasive developmental disorder, since these diagnoses are associated with more language delay. However, bear in mind that it is difficult to diagnose autism spectrum disorders at young ages. Many clinicians and physicians are reluctant to diagnose young children. Developmental growth is especially difficult to predict at very young ages, and children can change dramatically with early intervention. In particular, there may be reluctance to give a young child the diagnosis of autistic disorder, since it is hard to predict the course of the disorder, especially when responsiveness to treatment has yet to be determined. Nonetheless, in the hands of highly experienced clinicians, the sophisticated tools used to diagnose autism can be quite reliable when diagnosing young children, even as early as 18 months of age. Though challenging, diagnosis is important, as it can set a path for the early identification and intervention for individuals on the spectrum.

What Approach to Improving Communication Skills Is Recommended?

Over the years, a variety of approaches have been developed to help children with autism learn to comprehend and produce language. This book will focus on the approach that we, the authors, have used for a combined total of 45 years to help children with autism improve their communication skills—i.e., the Applied Behavior Analysis (ABA) approach.

If you are unfamiliar with ABA, think back to grade school when you first learned about the ***scientific method.*** Remember words like "observable," "data," "measurable," "hypothesis," and "experiment?" Remember projects like planting a seed and watching it grow (observation)? Remember collecting data on how much the plant grew or didn't grow (measurement) depending on what you did to it (water vs. no water; dark vs. exposure to sunlight (experimentation)? Well, ABA also involves using the scientific method. Applied Behavior Analysis is a science and branch of psychology that is concerned with the study of socially significant behaviors and with developing a technology of behavior change strategies. ABA seeks to intervene and improve behaviors and demonstrate (through the scientific method) a reliable relationship between their interventions and behavioral improvements.

The evidence supporting the use of ABA as a methodology to teach language and communication skills has an impressive, over-40-year history of research. In fact, perhaps one of the very reasons verbal behavior was first applied to individuals on the spectrum was to teach language and communication (Spradlin, 1963).

How This Book Is Organized

We have broken the book into several sections. We begin with a description of the common speech and language issues in children with autism. In Chapter 2, we then describe Skinner's Verbal Behavior classification system as an analytical tool for understanding and teaching language. In particular, we discuss how decisions about communication modality (do you speak, use sign language, gestures, or some kind of communication device?) are made in light of this conceptualization. The progression of our next chapters is based on the emergence and evolution of language (Emergence of Language, Building Language, Introduction to Social Language, and Strategies for Developing and Promoting the Use of Social Language).

We next address how to understand and change perseverative vocalizations and speech. The atypical use of vocalizations and words often poses as much difficulty for parents and teachers of children with autism as the appropriate use of vocalizations and words. Therefore, we wanted to address perseveration fully.

In addition, we have focused on a few special topics. We have included a chapter on fluency, a topic that has received a great deal of clinical attention in recent years. (A child's fluency often determines the success of his or her communications, since people must respond both appropriately and quickly to keep up with the pace of social interaction.) We have also addressed some of the communication issues that arise between children with autism and their siblings, since brothers and sisters are commonly involved in programs with young children with autism and since their adaptation is also important for the whole family.

Throughout the book, we have used many case examples to ensure that we focus on applying the techniques discussed. It is our hope that these examples make it easier to apply the concepts in individualized ways. We have chosen to use a wide array of children as examples, to convey the variability of the needs and characteristics of learners on the autism spectrum. As children with autism can be more different from than similar to each other, we wanted our examples to span their range of abilities and challenges. We hope to present you with information that can be useful to you regardless of the characteristics of the child(ren) you are trying to help and teach.

We believe this book will be useful for both parents and educators. While some sections of the book are more technical (e.g., perseverative speech, fluency), we have tried to balance that information with real-life examples of children we have known. We hope it provides a mixture of accurate and precise information on strategies and creative ideas for applications of those strategies.

References

American Psychiatric Association. (2000). *Diagnostic and Statistical Manual of Mental Disorders* (4th edition text revision). Washington, DC: Author.

Lord, C., Rutter, M., DiLavore, P., & Risi, S. (1999). *Autism Diagnostic Observation Schedule.* Los Angeles: Western Psychological Services.

Lovaas, O. I. (1987). Behavioral treatment and normal intellectual functioning in young autistic children. *Journal of Consulting and Clinical Psychology, 55,* 3-9.

Rutter, M., LeCouteur, A., & Lord, C. (2003). *Autism Diagnostic Interview-Revised.* Los Angeles: Western Psychological Services.

Smith T., McAdam, D., & Napolitano, D. (2007). Autism and applied behavior analysis. In P. Sturmey & A. Fitzer (Eds.), *Autism Spectrum Disorders: Applied Behavior Analysis, Evidence, and Practice* (pp. 1-29). Austin, TX: Pro-Ed.

Spradlin, J.E. (1963). Assessment of speech and language of retarded children: The Parsons language sample. *Journal of Speech and Hearing Disorder Monograph, 10,* 8-31.

Wing, L. (1988). The continuum of autistic disorders. In E. Schopler & G.M. Mesibov (Eds.), *Diagnosis and Assessment in Autism* (pp.91-110). New York: Plenum.

1 Issues in Speech and Language Development in Children with Autism

Clarissa

Clarissa is a two-year-old girl who was diagnosed with an autism spectrum disorder six months ago. Her parents had been concerned about her development since early in her infancy. She was their third child. At first, they labeled her as a low-maintenance baby, and marveled at how much less attention she appeared to need compared to their older children. However, as the months went on, they become mildly concerned. Clarissa didn't seem as interested in people as their other children had been. She didn't look at their faces as much, smile as consistently, or babble back and forth with them.

Clarissa's parents started mentioning these differences to their pediatrician when their daughter was about 6 months of age. By the time she was 12 months of age, they were concerned, and the pediatrician began to track her developmental milestones more specifically. In the months following Clarissa's first birthday, it became clear that she was exhibiting symptoms associated with the early diagnosis of an autism spectrum disorder. She did not point, follow her parents' point or gaze, and was not using words to express anything. Professionals said that Clarissa had "deficits in joint attention," meaning that she did not readily respond to requests by others to notice things in her environment. She also did not try to get others involved in noticing what she was observing or doing. (For example, she might be interested in a duck at the pond, but would not try to get her parents to notice it.) Furthermore, she seemed not to understand much of what was said to her.

Clarissa was referred for early intervention after her diagnosis. As part of EI, she received a combination of speech therapy and ABA intervention. Clarissa's response to treatment was not smooth. She engaged in severe tantrums whenever anyone interacted with her. She ran from the door whenever she saw a therapist coming. She clung to her mother when it was time to work with an instructor.

Clarissa was not able to imitate sounds or to make spontaneous speech sounds. She was also not able to understand instructions or to do basic skills such as matching identical objects. Her primary way of expressing herself was to throw herself on the floor and scream. She did this to express dissatisfaction (such as when a therapist came to work with her), but she also did it as a communication strategy. If she wanted TV or her Barbies or a snack, she threw herself on the floor in a tantrum. When she did this, her parents generally tried to guess what was bothering her, and would offer her a variety of items.

Joey

Joey is a three-and-a-half-year-old boy with autism. He was diagnosed at the age of two, and received intensive home-based therapy until the age of three. At age three, he entered a specialized preschool program that continued to focus on the development of skills in all relevant areas. He made substantial progress in many areas through intensive ABA intervention. He can now identify many common objects, imitate sequences of actions, and identify numbers and letters, and he also plays well with a variety of materials.

Communication, however, has been the most difficult and substantial challenge for Joey. Joey has trouble using his words to make his needs known. For example, he can identify water and answer the question "What is it?" when shown water. However, he doesn't ask for water, even when he is extremely thirsty. He also doesn't ask for other things he wants or needs, for help with difficult tasks, or for a break when he is frustrated. At these times, Joey is quite dependent on adults to notice his state of need. If they ask him what he wants at these times, he will answer and will then get access to the needed items. However, Joey's parents and instructors are well aware that such dependence will be limiting as Joey ages. They also recognize that Joey will not always have adults at his beck and call. They would like to help Joey develop some communication survival skills. Specifically, they want him to be able to ask for items and assistance as needed, without being prompted or reminded to do so by an adult in his environment.

Henry

Henry is five years old. He has responded beautifully to intervention for his autism spectrum disorder, and he does well in an included kindergarten setting. He still receives some targeted instruction at home, primarily to address issues in communication and in social skills.

Henry is very interested in other kids, and he often watches them. He knows how to play simple games like the kids on his block do, and they are often eager to include him. It can be hard, however, for him to keep up with them in play or in conversation. While he might be able to answer a simple question, he struggles when questions become more elaborate or abstract. For example, when asked to cover his eyes and count to ten before searching for his friends in hide and seek, he has difficulty carrying out all the steps and will go back to counting and closing his eyes several times. Other times, Henry does not know how to respond when children his age express opinions about their likes and dislikes of various food smells during lunch or talk about the costumes they will be wearing for Halloween ("Wow, cool Spiderman" or "Yikes, scary pirate—argh, Matey").

Sometimes, Henry's parents really wince when they see the other kids just continue playing without including him or find another kid to play more elaborately with. They realize that their son needs help in responding to his peers, in keeping a conversation going, and in attaching language to his play. They are just not sure where to begin.

Jake

Jake, age 8, is very adept at speaking clearly and articulately on a wide variety of topics. As a young child, his speech and language skills seemed to develop on a typical timetable, and even seemed advanced in some respects because of the sophisticated knowledge he possessed about highly specific topics such as plumbing. However, Jake is not interested in speaking with others, unless the subject involves pipes and plumbing (his special interest). He initiates conversations on these topics, but if a peer shifts the topic to something else, Jake simply walks away.

Young children with autism spectrum disorders have a wide range of communication skills. Clarissa, Joey, Henry, and Jake represent just four of the broad patterns of delays and difficulties that may occur:

- Clarissa exhibits many of the deficits associated with the youngest learners with autism, most notably an inability to get her wants and needs understood and an absence of learning readiness skills.
- Joey is a lot like many kids with autism. He responded well to intensive ABA intervention. He learned many basic skills, and is able to function well in a classroom environment. However, Joey does not spontaneously request things, and often passively waits for others to notice that he needs assistance.
- Henry has done extremely well in intervention. He can keep up with many of the academic requirements in school, and he demonstrates genuine social interest. However, he has difficulty in play situations that are more abstract and complex. He also struggles to continue conversation beyond simple exchanges. In short, Henry lacks the ability to engage in sustained and varied conversation and play.
- Jake has no difficulties in learning vocabulary words and producing the speech sounds of our language. However, he struggles with pragmatics of language and understanding the interests of others. Socially, Jake is at a huge disadvantage because he seems not to care about what his peers want to talk about and often doesn't notice that peers are turned off by his topics of conversation.

Common Problems with Communication Skills

Although each child on the autism spectrum is unique, most of them share at least some of the difficulties with speech and language illustrated above. As explained in the Introduction, diagnostically, impaired communication is a defining feature of autism. Although it is not known exactly why language acquisition goes awry with autism, some scientists have suggested that the neural connectivity in the brain may be abnormal (Groen et al., 2008).

Young children on the autism spectrum may have difficulties with some or all of the aspects of communication skills discussed in the sections below.

Language Comprehension

Language comprehension (also referred to as ***receptive language***) is the key to success at home, at school, and in the community. If a child does not understand what is said to him, he has trouble following directions, responding to inquiries, and making sense of the world. For instance, a peer may ask the child with autism, "Did you ever go roller skating? We went to a rink near my house and it was cool." If the child is overwhelmed with the language presented, he may make no reply or may simply say, "roller skates." Others may believe that someone who has poor comprehension is noncompliant, oblivious, uninterested, or rude.

Over the years, many theories as to why language comprehension is difficult for people with autism have been presented by researchers and clinicians. Three popular theories—Weak Central Coherence, Executive Dysfunction theory, and the Social Inference Theory (Martin & McDonald, 2003)—have been the most studied and are described below. Researchers are beginning to understand that language comprehension in individuals with autism involves a range of difficulties in pragmatic understanding and that there is probably an interplay of many mechanisms (such as the different ones described by each theory) and cognitive abilities that account for the range of deficits in language comprehension. Of the three theories cited above, the Social Inference Theory (also known as Theory of Mind) has received the most attention.

Table 1-1 | Theories about Language Comprehension Difficulties

Theory	Deficit
Weak Central Coherence Hypothesis	Suggests that language comprehension and pragmatic difficulties exist because of the individual's inability to use context to derive meaning. That is, the person cannot integrate information into a "whole" and attends to small pieces of information instead.
Executive Dysfunction Theory	Proposes that the brain has disordered frontal lobe functioning which is responsible for driving motivation, planning, concept formation, inferential and abstract reasoning, and considering "rules" of conversation change in context.
The Social Inference Theory	Suggests that the individual has a deficit in the ability to infer the mental states of others. Also known as Theory of Mind (ToM).

Figurative language can be especially difficult for many children with autism spectrum disorders to understand, even if they have relatively good basic language comprehension skills. One reason for this is because of the literal or concrete thinking that takes place with individuals on the autism spectrum. For example, if someone were to say, "I'm so nervous about my first date, I have butterflies in my stomach," an individual with autism could potentially misunderstand this statement to literally mean there are butterflies flying around in the person's stomach. Or, another example, if a teacher says, "Everyone, sit criss, cross, applesauce," a child without knowledge of that specific instruction may not even interpret that statement as an instruction.

Difficulties in understanding the use of pronouns can also be especially pronounced and noticeable for children on the autism spectrum. For example, a child may say "YOU want a cookie" to mean "I want a cookie."

Language Production

This is the area of communication that speech-language pathologists refer to as "expressive language." It involves conveying a message (via speech, sign language, writing, symbols, etc.) to others in a way they can understand. Young children with autism can have difficulties with a number of language production skills, including these speech skills defined in Table 1-2:

- articulation (sometimes related to apraxia, see below),
- phonology,
- volume,
- prosody,
- modulation,
- semantics (can affect receptive language, as well)
- syntax (can affect receptive language, as well)

Oscar spoke at such a low volume that he could not be understood by peers. In fact, his classmates thought he was nonverbal, as they had never been able to hear him communicate effectively with them.

Those who do not yet speak can also struggle with language production issues. For example, a child who is being taught sign language as an alternative communication method may have difficulties using his hands to form recognizable signs. Or someone who is learning to use an electronic communication device may have trouble learning which word/symbol to choose to communicate his needs and wants.

Apraxia

There is some evidence that difficulties with language production in children with autism spectrum disorders are sometimes associated with apraxia. ***Apraxia*** (which may also be referred to as ***dyspraxia***) refers to difficulties in executing learned, purposeful movements. Apraxia is not due to muscle weakness, comprehension deficits, sensory difficulties (such as hearing loss), or intellectual disabilities.

There are three main forms of apraxia (Sattler & Hoge, 2006). Two of them may affect a child's ability to sequence the movements needed to speak. ***Bucco-facial apraxia*** is an impaired ability to perform facial movements on command such as protruding the tongue, puckering the lips, or sniffing in response to commands. (Sometimes, however, the person can make these movements spontaneously.) ***Imitative apraxia*** is the impaired ability to repeat actions performed by others despite adequate motor control of limbs. Apraxia may affect children differently at different times. Sometimes a child may produce

Table 1-2 | Linguistic Terms

Articulation: refers to the adjustments and movements of speech organs such as the tongue, lips, and palate involved in pronouncing a particular sound. It is also the act of articulating speech.

Modulation: refers to the use of stress or pitch in a particular construction of speech such as the use of rising pitch in, "I want a cookie now!" It is an important element of prosody.

Phonology: refers to the perception and production of sound units and how sounds such as those of each letter in the alphabet are organized and used in language. It is the systematic use of sound to encode meaning in any spoken language. For example, "thr" as in "three" or "through" is a valid sound in English, but "thb" is not.

Prosody: deals with the rhythmic melody of speech such as intonation, stress, and pitch and involves the use of gestures during speech. Prosody often conveys the speaker's emotion, such as when adding emphasis or stress to a particular utterance (e.g., I want the BIG cookie!). It can also convey whether an utterance is meant as a statement, question, or command (e.g., I want the big cookie; I want the big cookie?, or I want the big cookie!) or can help convey the speaker's meaning (e.g., She's my MOTHER vs. SHE'S my mother).

Semantics: refers to the meaning of words (lexical) and items, and can also refer to a range of ideas. For example, the words cat, kitty, and meow could all be used to convey the same meaning, but would be best understood when in context. Semantic skills are important for understanding language in social context. For example, someone who was just familiar with the dictionary meaning of "down" would not understand the slang expression "Are you down with it?" to mean "do you agree?" Semantic skills also enable us to keep up with how word meanings change over time (e.g., most Americans no longer use "gay" as a synonym for happy).

Syntax: refers to the structure of words in sentences and the rules that govern the way words combine to form phrases, clauses, and sentences. Syntax is a major component of grammar. It is important to understand that rules that govern syntax can be distinct from the meanings that words may convey. That is, you may have a perfectly correct grammatical statement, but it may not be comprehensible. Noam Chomsky, a language development expert, wrote the following sentence to emphasize this point, "Colorless green ideas sleep furiously."

a word correctly on one occasion, but then not be able to say it again. Other children with apraxia may be able to say short words correctly, but stumble over longer ones, or may be able to say single words, but cannot put them together into a sentence.

Pragmatics

Perhaps a defining characteristic of autism spectrum disorders is difficulty in using language appropriately and in social contexts. This is an area of communication skills referred to as pragmatics.

Most young children with autism spectrum disorders have great difficulty understanding and following the conventions and rules governing the use of language for social communication. As a result, they frequently have trouble with pragmatics skills such as:

- greeting;
- demanding or requesting;
- changing their language according to the needs of the listener or situation (e.g., talking differently to a baby than to an adult); and
- following rules for conversations such as staying on topic, turn-taking, and using verbal and nonverbal signals, facial expressions, and eye-contact.

They can also have difficulties using the speech skills they do have in socially acceptable and meaningful ways. For example, many young children with autism spectrum disorders have perseverative speech (they get "stuck" on a word, phrase, or topic and repeat it inappropriately). This is such a significant problem that it is discussed in detail in Chapter 8.

All four children introduced at the beginning of this chapter have some difficulties with pragmatics:

- Clarissa lacks many of the most basic skills needed to engage others in communication, including functional speech and requesting skills, basic receptive understanding skills, and appropriate eye-contact.
- Joey does not know how to request appropriately even though he can talk; he also relies too much on adults before communicating.
- Henry has excellent speech but falls apart when it comes to keeping a conversation going with his peers or using language when engaged in play.
- Jake's primary problems with communication skills are in the area of pragmatics. Although he can speak fluently, he perseverates on a topic (plumbing) that others find boring and bizarre and he cannot read their nonverbal and verbal signals that they would like to talk about something else.

Assessing Speech and Language Difficulties

Given the wide range and varying degree of language difficulties and deficits that children with autism are likely to have, intervention must be highly individualized. Treatment should focus on relevant aspects of functional language that are most important to the individual child. A comprehensive assessment of language skills is necessary. Communication assessments entail a thorough analysis of skills in all aspects of communication—understanding, ability to produce language, and ability to convey information to others effectively. A major focus of this assessment is the functional use of language.

In general, an experienced behavior analyst, teacher, educator, or other professional working with your child is likely to perform (at a minimum) a broad communication/language assessment that may use both standardized and nonstandardized tools. This is done to help the person and team get started on working on some communication/language goals with your child, as well as to document what his baseline (beginning) skills are.

If your child was formally diagnosed with an autism spectrum disorder, you were likely asked questions about language development or had to fill out a paper and pencil inventory of your child's communication and adaptive skills. If it is recommended that a more thorough speech and language evaluation be conducted, you will typically be referred to a speech-language pathologist for one. It is highly recommended that the person assessing your child also have experience assessing children with autism spectrum disorders.

The good news is that you do not have to complete a thorough speech and language evaluation or wait weeks and months before you can begin intervention with your child. Often, a good observation by an experienced professional is sufficient for the professional to make some quick recommendations regarding communication skills your child needs to learn. In fact, many professionals will give parents some assignments and recommendations to carry out at home as they wait for a more detailed evaluation.

A few clinicians use state-of-the-art standardized assessments such as the Autism Diagnostic Interview (ADI; Rutter, LeCouteur, & Lord, 2003) and the Autism Diagnostic Observation Scale (ADOS; Lord, Rutter, DiLavore, & Risi, 1999). The ADOS, in particular, represents a large step forward in the assessment of individuals with autism, as it is based on direct observation. It also was developed to capture deficits in some of the subtle characteristics of children with autism, such as joint attention, imaginary play, and reciprocal conversation.

Other specialized (but nonstandardized) assessments that can be very useful in evaluating the speech and language skills of children with autism spectrum disorders are the Assessment of Basic Language and Learner Skills (ABLLS; Partington & Sundberg, 1998) and ABLLS-R (Partington, 2006), which are assessments of task-analyzed skills across many areas of development, including communication skills. Also see Chapter 4 for information on the VB MAPP.

Unfortunately, relatively few diagnosticians are familiar with diagnostic assessments such as the ADOS, which can delay obtaining a definitive diagnosis, especially when symptoms are subtle or confusing in their presentation. If you are interested in finding a professional who specializes in the evaluation and diagnosis of autism spectrum disorders, you might want to check out major hospitals, universities, and autism excellence centers in your area, as well as private practitioners. It is recommended that you specifically ask if the professionals assessing your child will administer an ADOS or other standardized diagnostic tool and if they have experience assessing children diagnosed with autism.

Table 1-3 | Developmental "Red Flags" in Communication

This table summarizes some of the most common and obvious differences in the development of communication skills in children with autism spectrum disorders. It was adapted from *Demystifying Autism Spectrum Disorders: A Guide to Diagnosis for Parents and Professionals* (Bruey, 2004).

By Age Two: You want to see...	**"Red flags" that may suggest an autism spectrum disorder**
■ Child shows a wide range of facial expressions, including big smiles directed toward others during social interactions.	■ Facial expressions tend to be unanimated and smiles that do occur are usually not directly related to social interactions.
■ Child initiates and sustains eye contact. ■ Child is often looking to others' eyes for information.	■ Eye contact is brief and rarely initiated. Child may tend to look at others or objects via peripheral vision (i.e., out of the corner of his eye). ■ Child may seem to look beyond you.
■ Child responds to own name when called.	■ Child inconsistently responds to own name being called. (Parents often worry that the child is deaf.)
■ Child is beginning to use basic gestures such as pointing, putting arms in the air to indicate a wish to be picked up, putting finger to lips while saying "Shhh," etc.	■ Child doesn't use basic gestures to communicate needs or wants. Instead, the child may whine or cry without any awareness that others need more information to discern his needs. ■ Often, there is an absence of waving and of pointing. These are often the first signs noted in the 12- and 15-month checkups.
■ Child begins to speak in one-word sentences that are communicative in nature; i.e., the child is clearly attempting to communicate with others rather than just babbling.	■ Speech is absent or delayed. Sometimes child's speech may develop appropriately but is generally uncommunicative (e.g., he may repeat dialogues from videos to himself; may talk without *intent* to communicate to others). ■ Alternatively, the child may lose speech, babbling, or social skills that have developed.

■ Child begins to bring objects to others or point out objects to share enjoyment or interest (e.g., points to a cow while making eye contact and says, "Cow!")	■ Child tends to bring objects to others only when assistance is needed (e.g., brings cup when thirsty or broken toy that needs fixing). ■ The child may take someone by the wrist and lead them to a desired object but then let go as soon as the person's purpose has been served. ■ Child may use another person's hand as a tool (e.g., holds mom's finger to point in a book or grabs mom's hand to open door).
■ Child is able to engage in various imitative and reciprocal interactions and games such as Peek-a-Boo and Wheels on the Bus.	■ Child shows minimal ability to imitate the actions of others and social reciprocity is low or absent.

Other "Red Flags" to Look for in Young Children...

- Echolalia; that is, repeating words or phrases that the child has heard. This could involve repeating words immediately (e.g., when you ask him, "Do you want a cookie?," he responds, "Do you want a cookie?") or at a later time (repeating dialogue from videos that he's watched previously).
- Expressive speech may involve repeating the same words or phrases over and over again to himself or others (known as "perseverative speech"). Some children use *word salads* (combinations of real words strung together with no meaning) or made-up, meaningless words known as *neologisms*.
- The child may have difficulty understanding and following simple instructions. Sometimes the child is extremely inconsistent in responding to instructions, or may seem to follow them "when in the mood."
- Inability to "warm up" to others, no matter how much time has passed.
- For children aged five or older, there is difficulty taking others' perspective and understanding that other people don't think or feel exactly as they do. (Keep in mind that even children under five years who are typically developing have difficulty with this concept.)

An Overview of Treatment Using an ABA Approach

Who Will Work with Your Child?

When a child is receiving ABA treatment, he will have a team of professionals working with him to figure out what he needs to learn and help him with his learning goals/outcomes. The team will develop a program for him, detailing the goals/outcomes for him in various areas and spelling out who will work on these goals with your child and how frequently.

The types of professionals who might be on a team for a young child with ASD include:

- teachers,
- paraprofessionals,
- behavior analysts,
- psychologists,
- speech and language therapists,
- occupational therapists, and
- other professionals.

It is important for parents to understand that if your child receives early intervention services, sometimes professionals have unique titles because of the category of work they fall under according to state criteria. Typically, licensed and/or certified professionals such as behavior analysts, speech-language pathologists, psychologists, or occupational therapists are easily identified with their licenses or certifications. It gets tricky when you run into titles such as "developmental specialist," "behavior specialist," "assistant teacher," or "developmental interventionist." These are made-up titles that are given based on some kind of criteria the state and/or agency might set (e.g., experience working with children ages birth to eight, plus coursework in behavioral psychology may qualify an individual for a "behavior specialist" title).

As team members and advocates for their child, parents often have strong opinions as to who they want on a team. It is important to recognize that different professions bring different perspectives, strengths, and weaknesses to a program. Most importantly, all team members should recognize when consultation by licensed or formally certified professionals is needed. For example, if your child receives ABA therapy for several weeks without much progress, when should the team call in a speech therapist or psychologist to assess a specific skill?

Multipronged Approaches to Overcoming Language Issues: Comprehension, Context, and Communication

Your child's ABA team will take a multipronged approach to helping him overcome his difficulties with communication skills. Generally, they will try to boost your child's understanding of verbal and non-verbal communication while also helping him improve his expressive abilities. And they will figure out ways to weave this learning into daily life, so that communication makes sense to him in various contexts.

Just as learning doesn't happen in a vacuum, neither does language development. This is particularly important when thinking of children with autism who may have good speech production, but poor understanding of what is being said or asked of them as well as poor use of language (especially in functional contexts). For example, many children engage in perseverative speech, which may be excellent in production quality but poor in functionality. (We address perseverative speech extensively later in the book.)

With children who have good speech skills, it is very important to ensure that they also comprehend what others say to them. A good starting place for young learners is the day-to-day contexts of their lives. Teaching should be tailored to the child's experiences and the settings where he plays and learns. For example, a child who is under the age of three and receives early intervention services in the home encounters different stimuli (including language) than a 4- or 5-year-old who goes to preschool every day. Each child's physical location and day-to-day routines should influence which language concepts are targeted for instruction. For example, Nate, who receives early intervention services at home, might not need to know what a lunchbox, smock, and calendar are. However, Simon, who is a preschooler, would benefit from knowing the names of these items, the contexts they are used in, and related information about them. Embedding language in specific contexts is very important, particularly for the generalization and maintenance of skills.

The teaching format that an instructor uses is influenced by both characteristics of the child and the nature of the task. For example, some children may learn new words easily, after hearing the words several times in appropriate contexts. Emma, for instance, may understand the word "door" after hearing her parents say "open the door" several times. Another child may require many structured (discrete) trials to learn what the item is, and then later generalize the knowledge to the natural environment. For example, Megan might need to be formally taught the word "apple" by having an instructor or parent sit face to face with her, hold up a real apple, point to it, and say, "Apple" several times. Some children may respond well in the natural environment, yet be unable to demonstrate the skill in a more formal assessment. This may result from a problem in generalization or from difficulties in attention.

Sometimes a child appears to understand a word just because the context gives him a hint that helps him select an item correctly. For example, consider a child who is standing in front of the closet with his jacket on and is told, "Get your shoes." When he gets his shoes, it is possible that he is not responding to the spoken words, but rather to the contextual clues. In his experience, when he has his jacket and coat on, he must also put on his shoes. The problem is that these words will also occur in contexts in which cues are not available. (One must know "shoe" and what to do with shoes even when shoes are referred to outside of the routine of preparing to go out.) It is therefore important to ensure that the child is paying attention to the words that are spoken, and can comprehend them under many conditions. These conditions include the natural environment (i.e., routine contexts) and more structured (i.e., nonroutine) contexts in which additional contextual cues may not be available.

In ABA language treatment for very young children with autism, we often recommend teaching words first in context, and then gradually out of context. This is not a prescription, however, and sometimes we do it the opposite way.

Another important variable to consider when teaching language is the use of prompting strategies. Typically we want to use what is called a ***controlling prompt*** because it offers the fastest and easiest way to help the child respond to the stimulus that is presented and it "controls" the correct response. For example, often children with echolalia will repeat part of the direction the adult uses to cue a response. That is, they say the word "say" when you are asking them to "Say apple." Sometimes children also repeat the tail end of the question, such as when you ask a child, "What do you like to eat?" and prompt them to say, "apple" you get, "Eat, say apple." To overcome this issue, we may use a visual stimulus as a controlling prompt. For example, we may hold an actual apple or picture of an apple in front of the child at the right moment.

A trial would look something like this for a child prone to echolalia:

Therapist: "What do you like to eat? Say 'apple.'"

Child: "Say Apple" [incorrect response, should only say "apple"].

Therapist: "What do you like to eat? Say 'apple'" (holding up a picture of an apple or an actual apple).

Child: "Say apple."

Therapist: "What do you like to eat?" Therapist holds an apple in hand and shows the child a picture of an apple, but does not use a verbal prompt.

Child: "Apple."

As with any prompt, a major goal is to decrease the amount of prompts as quickly as possible so that the child is responding independently and does not become dependent on prompts.

Issues with Language Production

Your child's ABA program will also address difficulties with expressive language. Many young children with autism are helped to pronounce, articulate, or modulate speech sounds through the use of various types of prompting procedures. Clever strategies have been developed through the use of visual, auditory, and tactile cues to shape speech and teach children how to stress syllables, how to pronounce words, how to speak at different volumes, and how to coordinate their speech with other social gestures.

It should be noted that research does not support the practice of nonspeech oral-motor exercises to promote speech production in children with ASD (Lof & Watson, 2008; Powell, 2008). The practice of oral-motor exercises assumes that weak muscles of the mouth need to be strengthened, which will then increase the clarity of speech (Bunton, 2008; Powell, 2008). Many exercises are designed to increase strength, stamina, or range of motion. (Common ones include blowing horns and holding weighted sticks between the lips.) While the theory is appealing, it simply has not been supported by research. Unfortunately, the exercises remain popular and are commonly used with children on the autism spectrum. When considering a program or therapist for your child, be sure to ask whether nonspeech oral-motor exercises are emphasized, as these exercises may reduce time spent on more communicative means of language.

Helpful strategies for improving articulation, syllabic emphasis, and modulation of speech include the use and emphasis of various auditory cues, visual cues, pacing techniques, and tactile modalities, discussed below.

Strategies That Use Sensory Modalities

The strategies used to promote better speech production in ABA programs generally involve accentuating or highlighting one of the senses in such a way that they prompt the child to make a desired word or sound. The types of prompts chosen are often based on the child's strengths that are revealed through assessment (e.g., is he a visual learner? an auditory learner?), as well as on their effectiveness in prompting the child to respond.

Auditory Strategies

Auditory strategies involve using sounds or words that prompt a response. The example below describes some of the types of auditory strategies that may be helpful for young children with autism spectrum disorders:

Simon, a 34-month-old boy diagnosed with autism, had difficulty expressing certain consonant-vowel sounds involving two-syllable words such as "hippo" or "baby." His ABA team decided to use a vocal imitation program with Simon. They started by choosing several words that would be functional in Simon's environment. Since Simon loved animals and had a new baby sibling, the team chose to work on the names for

Simon's preferred animals and on labeling "baby" to refer to his sister. When only vocal imitation for the word "Hippo" was used, Simon would easily fill in "PO" after the instructor initially said "Hip," but Simon had difficulty imitating the full word, "Hippo." He often said, "Bippo." The team began to worry that he would practice errors. Interestingly, Simon was able to repeat, "Hi (short i sound) and "Po" when each syllable was discretely presented and broken down, but it was very hard for him to connect the syllables.

The team experimented with auditory cues such as holding the first syllable for a few seconds, until Simon began to say "Hi" (short i sound) and then added "Po." Simon had some success with this strategy at first, but kept reverting back to "Bippo." The team then decided to silently mouth the first syllable "Hi." This helped Simon pay attention to the instructor's mouth, thus helping Simon say the entire word correctly.

Visual Strategies

A visual strategy can be anything visual that the individual sees and that helps in evoking a response. Visual strategies can also serve as prompts.

Seeing a picture often helps children to produce words accurately and the strategy is easy to fade out later. For example, holding up a picture of a cat and asking the child to say "cat" can help him produce the appropriate sounds or word. For children who can read, showing the word "cat" (textual cue) can also be considered a visual strategy and can be quite helpful.

Sometimes strategies that combine a visual and a tactile component are used. For example, having the child draw a finger along a solid line or tap out the number of syllables to a word using blocks helps children with ASD to improve their language production.

Tactile Strategies

Tactile strategies involve having the child touch something to help him with language production. For example, if the child is working on the consonant-vowel sounds "be" (long "e" sound), he might be prompted to draw his finger on a solid dark line for five inches while saying the long "e" sound. Or if working on C-V-C-V (consonant-vowel-consonant-vowel) sounds such as "mama," the child might be asked to touch two blocks that are equally spaced apart, emphasizing the repetition of syllables.

What to Expect of Your Child in an ABA Program

There is good news for parents whose young children with ASD are involved in an ABA program. Research has consistently indicated that the earlier behavioral intervention starts, the better the prognosis is for that child. Communication will increase and your child will learn. It goes without saying that everyone on your child's team would like to see the best and most optimal progress for your child. In our experience, we have never met a child who could not learn or who could not gain socially significant skills that enhanced his life.

Autism is currently considered a life-long disorder; however, we also know that outcomes can vary tremendously, just as the diagnosis itself varies along a spectrum in terms of degree of disability. There are many variables that affect a child's progress. They include:

- intensive and early behavioral services,
- rate of learning,
- intellectual ability,
- rate of verbal imitation, and
- parent involvement (among others).

We have found that parents who focus on aspects of treatment that are within their control fare better than those who focus on things beyond their control.

Perhaps the most important message we can impart is to obtain good, intensive behavioral services as early as you can. Just remember, your child will make progress!

References

Bruey, C. T. (2004). *Demystifying Autism Spectrum Disorders: A Guide to Diagnosis for Parents and Professionals.* Bethesda, MD: Woodbine House.

Bunton, K. (2008). Speech versus nonspeech: Different tasks, different neural organization. *Seminars in Speech and Language, 29,* 267-75.

Groen, W. B., Zwiers, M. P., van der Gaag, R-J, & Buitelaar, J.K. (2008). The phenotype and neural correlates of language in autism: An integrative review. *Neuroscience and Biobehavioral Reviews 32,* 1416-25.

Lof, G. L. & Watson, M.M. (2008). A nationwide survey of nonspeech oral motor exercise use: Implications for evidence-based practice. *Language, Speech and Hearing Service in the Schools, 39,* 392-407.

Oller, D.K., Eilers, R.E., Neal, A.R., & Cobo-Lewis, A.B. (1998). Late onset of canonical babbling: A possible early marker of abnormal development. *American Journal on Mental Retardation, 103,* 249-63.

Powell, T. W. (2008). An integrated evaluation of nonspeech oral motor treatments. *Language, Speech and Hearing Services in the Schools, 39,* 422-27.

Sattler, J. M. & Hoge, R. D. (2006). *Assessment of Children: Behavioral, Social and Clinical Foundations.* 5th ed. La Mesa, CA: Jerome M. Sattler, Publisher, Inc.

2 Verbal Behavior: Understanding How and Why We Communicate

As explained in the Introduction, this book focuses on using ABA techniques to help young children with autism spectrum disorders improve their communication skills. To use this approach, it is essential to be able to analyze and interpret communicative acts as *behaviors*. In particular, you will need to understand the terminology and concepts related to the study of verbal behavior. With that foundation, you will be able to understand how and why decisions are made about selecting an alternative method of communication, such as signs or the Picture Exchange Communication System (PECS), if a child has difficulty using speech to communicate.

What Is Verbal Behavior?

You undoubtedly have a general understanding of the meaning of the word *behavior.* We generally use the word to refer to any action an individual does that has an impact on her environment or on the people and things in that environment. For example, if I kick a can down the sidewalk, that's behavior. Or if I pick up the can and put it in a trash can, that's behavior. But note that behavior is something that can be observed by others, so that what I am thinking when I decide to kick the can is *not* a behavior.

According to the ABA definition of behavior, a behavior is an action that can be reinforced, punished, and otherwise affected by environmental events. So, if I hurt my foot when I kick the can, I will perceive that as a punishment and probably stop kicking it. Likewise, if my spouse frowns at me when I kick the can, I may interpret that as a punishment and stop my behavior. I will then be less likely to kick cans when out in public with him. But if he laughs and joins in, I will likely find his response reinforcing and be more likely to kick the next can I see. I might also repeat my can-kicking behavior if I'm out by myself and enjoy the sound the can makes as it skids along the sidewalk.

Verbal behavior is a special type of behavior originally defined by B.F. Skinner, who published a book entitled *Verbal Behavior* in 1957. B. F. Skinner is the most well-known behavior analyst and was a major contributor to the science of behavior, both in his research and in his theoretical writings. His analysis of verbal behavior is one of his theoretical contributions. Skinner posited that verbal behavior was just like other behaviors, in that it could be reinforced and punished and affected by environmental events. He thought verbal behavior was distinct from other behavior, though, because it involved behavior in which reinforcement was only mediated by another person. In other words, verbal behavior is a social process. It does not involve a person simply interacting with his or her environment. It involves a person interacting with another person, a *listener* who receives the communication.

In other words, a child who wants apple juice may go to the cabinet and take an apple juice box. This is behavior; the child is interacting with the environment. Alternately, the child may find her parent and ask for apple juice. The parent may then get the juice and bring it to the child. This is verbal behavior. The reinforcement (juice) is mediated by another person (the parent).

Children can "ask" a parent for juice in many different ways. They may vocally request some by saying, "Can I have juice?" They might sign for juice. They might exchange a picture to request juice. They might simply take a parent's hand and place it on the cupboard. They might take a parent to the refrigerator and then begin to have a tantrum. All of these behaviors would meet Skinner's definition and concept of verbal behavior.

The *form* of the behavior (sign, PECS, vocalization, tantrum) does not affect whether or not it is a verbal behavior. Instead, what matters in determining whether a behavior is a verbal behavior or not is the *function* of the behavior. In the examples in the previous paragraph, the function of the behavior is requesting (although Skinner used a different word that will be explained below).

Skinner was not interested in how language should be taught or in how children with autism should be taught language. He was not writing about those topics. He was writing about language in general, in a theoretical way. However, in recent years, his work has been examined for its application and usefulness in teaching language to individuals with autism.

If your child is in an ABA program, you will likely encounter a verbal behavior approach to teaching language skills. It will help you to learn about the different functions of verbal behaviors so you can understand your child's strengths and weaknesses with each, and help your child's team in selecting language and communication behaviors to improve.

Functions of Verbal Behavior

Skinner's focus on the function of verbal behavior stemmed from his analysis of communication. He noted that communications have many different functions. We might say things to request an item, to convey something we see, or to answer a question. For example, I might say "coffee" to a coworker who is pouring coffee, meaning I would like a cup as well. This is a request. I might say "coffee" as I walk by my coworker brewing a pot, conveying that I smell the coffee. In this case, I am simply labeling something I am experiencing from a sensory perspective. Someone might ask me, "What's your favorite beverage to drink in the morning?" I would say "coffee." In this case, I am just having a conversation; I am neither requesting nor labeling something in my environment.

In each of these instances, the function of my communication is different. Skinner wanted to describe the functions of communication, in an effort to analyze and understand the complex world of verbal behavior. He classified each function (which he referred to as ***verbal operants***) separately, and gave them names. The names he gave them were not existing words. Rather, he developed new terms, which would not be associated with our preconceived notions. (A few of the most commonly cited ones are described below. If you want to be fully informed about verbal behavior, we encourage you to read Skinner's analysis and some of the resources listed at the end of the chapter.)

Mands: Skinner used the label ***mand*** to describe a situation in which someone is conveying a desire for something and asking another person to give us that item (i.e., requesting). Manding involves states of emotional desire that are satisfied by receiving specific reinforcement. In other words, the request for coffee is satisfied by the receipt of coffee; the request for juice is satisfied by the receipt of juice. Skinner called such requests mands because the person is issuing a com*mand,* and making a de*mand* of others.

Tacts: Skinner used the term ***tact*** to describe situations in which a person is describing something he or she is experiencing on a sensory level. If someone is sharing information about what he or she is hearing, seeing, smelling, or tasting, it is called a tact. Skinner chose the term tact because the person is making con*tact* with the environment when this occurs.

Echoics: Skinner described another type of verbal behavior in which the person simply responds to the verbal behavior of another with verbal behavior that matches it identically. For example, I say "banana," and you say "banana." In the work of teaching children with autism, we usually call this ***verbal imitation.*** Skinner labeled this kind of verbal behavior an ***echoic.***

Intraverbals: Skinner also described many different circumstances in which people are communicating, but are not manding or tacting. They may be discussing things that are not physically present—events that occurred over the weekend, an upcoming vacation, or a movie they saw the previous night. In fact, this kind of conversation occurs quite frequently in each of our lives. It is the daily reciprocal, back-and-forth conversational exchange that constitutes much of our social interaction. Skinner called this kind of verbal behavior an ***intraverbal.*** Intraverbals involve responding to the verbal behavior of another with content that does not identically match it (as echoics do).

The Relevance of Verbal Behavior to Children with Autism

What does the analysis of verbal behavior have to do with young children with autism spectrum disorder?

The short answer is that ABA techniques have been proven to be very effective in helping children with autism learn new skills and generalize them to many different environments. And at the heart of ABA is the need to define which behaviors need to change and then measure how behaviors change in response to intervention. Skinner's ideas about analyzing verbal behavior allow us to quantify and measure communication skills and changes in those skills over time in the same way that we measure and graph other behaviors. With verbal behavior, we specifically track and graph the verbal operants (mands, tacts, intraverbals, and echoics) discussed above.

As a parent and team member, you want to make sure that your child's usage of each operant is being tracked and that your child is developing functional skills related to communication. Remember, just because your child can say "juice" when she sees juice (a tact) doesn't mean that she also knows how to ask (mand) for juice, talk about the juice (intraverbal), or repeat "juice" (echoic) when asked. If you understand verbal behavior and the functions of language, you can help ensure that your child meets her targets for language learning and develops a good conceptual base regarding language functions.

Researchers have found that the mand, the tact, the intraverbal, and the echoic have tremendous relevance for learners on the autism spectrum (Sundberg, 2007; Sundberg & Michael, 2001; Sundberg & Partington, 1999; Partington & Sundberg, 1998). Skinner described and defined other functions of communication (verbal operants) as well, but these are the ones that have been described the most in the application of his work to teaching language to children with autism.

One reason for this resurgence of interest in verbal behavior is that most children with autism have severe language deficits in one or more of these areas. Most children with autism do not mand well. They may request only a very few items, they may request in ways that are unclear and ineffective, and they may fail to mand spontaneously (Sundberg, 2004). They rarely label items in the environment in an effort to share their experience. Any tacting they engage in is generally prompted by inquiries from others. Reciprocal conversations (intraverbals) are also a very significant challenge. Many children with autism cannot take part in conversation, or can engage only in limited and brief exchanges, often on a restricted range of topics. Articulation and pacing issues make it necessary for many children with autism to practice verbal imitation (echoic training) extensively.

In addition, children with autism do not necessarily transfer language across functions smoothly (Hall & Sundberg, 1987; Lamarre & Holland, 1985; Michael, 1982). They may be able to label an item, yet never request it. For example, if you hold up a bottle of water and ask "What is it?", the child may say "water." But she may not ask for water, even when extremely thirsty. This difficulty in transferring language across functions makes it necessary for us to program for each verbal operant (function of communication).

Skinner's analysis reminds us to program for language acquisition comprehensively across the different functions of verbal behavior. That is, the child's team will identify each function of communication that is difficult for her and develop goals (targets) and intervention plans for each problem area. For example, often mands are taught first because they enable a child to get her immediate needs and desires met and reduce frustration. This is in contrast to the way speech/language therapy is usually approached for children who have communication difficulties due to other types of disabilities. For example, if a child with Down syndrome or cerebral palsy is having difficulty with language skills (and she can already use language functionally), therapy might focus on helping the child master new vocabulary, grammatical rules, or parts of speech such as verbs, pronouns, or prepositions rather than on the broad functions of communication that she struggles with.

Misconceptions Regarding Verbal Behavior

There has been a tremendous amount of confusion about Verbal Behavior in the last few years, as it has received more attention in educating students with autism. The main misconception has to do with understanding it as an analytical tool vs. an instructional approach. As mentioned above, Skinner did not comment on how language would be taught, and did not have any application to children with autism in mind. He was simply designing an analytical tool that would help to understand verbal behavior in general. Essentially, he developed a classification system to describe the functions of language.

However, in application, many people describe doing a "verbal behavior" program. This really does not make sense, given what "verbal behavior" refers to—this analytical approach and/or classification system. Clinicians who have adopted the use of Skinner's classification system often do teach in a certain way—for example, they provide fast-paced instruction and they mix different targets of instruction in their teaching sessions. However, these strategies actually have nothing to do with verbal behavior or with the use of Skinner's analysis of verbal behavior to teach language.

Often when parents hear about the "verbal behavior program," they want it to be used with their children. They may think that there is such a thing as "verbal behavior" instruction, and they may ask to have it instead of discrete trial instruction. Of course, as we just said above, "verbal behavior" does not refer to any particular approach. The analysis of verbal behavior can be combined and applied with any instructional approach, including discrete trial instruction. (Of course, we would want to ensure that the discrete trial instruction is also state-of-the-art. This means we would want to see it done with fast pacing and with the combination of new and mastered material. These are the elements mentioned above that are sometimes erroneously labeled as associated with verbal behavior. In fact, they are just state-of-the-art ABA instructional techniques.)

Sometimes parents and others do not even realize that the analysis of verbal behavior is part of Applied Behavior Analysis. Instead, they may think it's an alternative model of instruction, since it has not been used in the instruction of children with autism very long. Similarly, it is sometimes seen as "new ABA" in contrast to some approaches and applications that have been in use for longer periods of time. Behavior analysts need to do a better job describing the origins and definitions of Verbal Behavior!

A Note about Verbal Behavior as an Intervention

Much of what we have said in this chapter emphasizes that VB is a classification system and an analytic tool. All clinicians agree that Skinner said nothing about ***how to teach*** language, but was simply describing communication by its functions.

Although Verbal Behavior is not an instructional approach, it is commonly referred to as an "intervention," mainly because it has been paired with a wide variety of effective ABA tools. The combination of these approaches along with the Skinner's original classification system has come to define the intervention package. The use of the term Applied Verbal Behavior has helped to emphasize this evolution.

In addition, Mary Lynch Barbera's book, *The Verbal Behavior Approach: How to Teach Children with Autism and Related Disorders* (Barbera & Rasmussen, 2007), does a great deal to clarify these issues. She describes an ABA approach that utilizes Skinner's classification system to teach language, and that is especially well suited to children with minimal language abilities. Her book describes how the procedures commonly paired with the use of the classification system (e.g., Interspersal, fast pacing, errorless procedures, pairing) are effective in creating an environment in which communication is encouraged, engagement is maximized, frustration is minimized, and reinforcement is high.

In recent research, the apparent differences between more traditional approaches and the VB approach are becoming less obvious. In a 2010 symposium at the Association for Behavioral Analysis International, Dr. Philip Hineline concluded that the VB Approach and the traditional Lovaas DTI model were increasingly similar. It may be that traditional approaches are evolving in exactly the directions that the VB Approach/AVB Model have evolved. This reflects shared recognition of some of the essential needs of children with autism and the most effective interventions to address them.

For More Information: For readers interested in the evolution of the VB classification system as it applies to educational interventions for students with autism, here are two additional sources of information:

- In 2009, Andy Bondy was interviewed about VB in the Association for Behavior Analysis International's *Autism Special Interest Group Newsletter.* His interview covers several of the main controversies in VB and its application to autism, and reviews how PECS was developed with Skinner's classification system in mind. This interview can be accessed at: *www.autismpppsig.org/index.php?option=com_content&view=article&id=55&Itemid=53* (or go to *www.autismppsig.org* and search for "Andy Bondy").
- In 2010, *The Behavior Analyst Today* interviewed Andy Bondy, Mark Sundburg, and Barbara and John Esch on the issues, controversies, and considerations in the application of VB to individuals with autism. This in-depth series of interviews focuses on the commonly discussed

topics and the confusion that surrounds clinical practice. The article also includes a wealth of references regarding verbal behavior and related clinical practice questions. This series of interviews contained in Volume 11 (Number 3, pp. 186-205) can be accessed at www.baojournal.com/BAT%20Journal/BATissues.html.

What Is Discrete Trial Instruction?

As the name implies, discrete trial instruction is a teaching strategy that involves breaking skills down into separate (discrete) components and then teaching them over the course of many attempts (trials). In a teaching session, the teacher presents questions, requests, or tasks to the child, models the response for the child, if necessary, and prompts the child to respond, if necessary. If the child responds correctly, she is rewarded or *reinforced*. If the child does not respond correctly, she is corrected.

For example, a session aimed at teaching a child to label an "apple" might go like this:

Teacher: Holds a picture of an apple and says, "Apple."

Student: Says, "Apple."

Teacher: Says, "Great job" and provides a tangible reinforcer (toy car).

Or, if the student does not respond by saying "Apple," the teacher immediately prompts the correct answer by saying, "Say Apple" and systematically rewards the child for the prompted response. With each subsequent trial, the goal would be to work the response to a point of independence. That is, the child would say, "apple" without requiring a prompted answer. Depending on the child and her history of learning how to label, this skill might be acquired with a few trials or several hundred trials across several days.

Modality: Alternatives to Speech

Whenever we discuss communication in children with autism, we are automatically drawn into a discussion of communication modality. The ultimate goal for people with autism is to use speech for communication. Parents and educators alike agree on this as the most efficient and effective means of expression and interaction. Individuals who can develop vocal speech are much better able to navigate the social world, to function independently in the community, and to convey complicated needs and thoughts.

Many people with autism do become vocal communicators, but many do not (Bryson, 1996: Lord & Paul, 1997). Approximately 50 percent of individuals with an autism spectrum disorder develop some form of vocal communication.

When speech is not likely to be a sufficient or effective means of communication for an individual, alternative methods are generally considered. Some people with autism use these alternative modes of communication throughout their lives. Often, however, the alternative system is used as a bridge, until the person develops stronger speech skills.

The main alternative communication modalities discussed for children with autism spectrum disorders are sign language and the Picture Exchange Communication System (PECS). Sign language allows the child to communicate her wants and needs through gestures and other body movements. PECS teaches the child to communicate her wants and needs by exchanging a picture or sentence strip with a listener. In recent years, there has been tremendous controversy over which of these modalities is "better" for individuals with autism.

Many clinicians express strong opinions one way or the other, but most of those opinions are not based on an objective evaluation of data. Parents are often confused about which direction to go in, and often hear highly discrepant opinions from consultants involved with their child.

Fears of Introducing Alternative Means of Communicating

The decision to pursue an alternative means of communication is often controversial and emotional for parents, in particular. Many parents fear that allowing their child to use a communication method other than speech will reduce the likelihood that the child will speak. Parents often worry that the child will come to rely on the alternative system, and that her motivation to speak will be reduced. Parents may also fear that the child will use the other modality as a "crutch" and will not communicate via speech when she has an easier option.

In fact, using an alternative system has no negative impact on the development of speech. On the contrary, whether sign language or the Picture Exchange Communication System is used, there is evidence that speech becomes *more* likely with the use of an alternative communication modality (e.g., Ganz & Simpson, 2004; Ganz, Simpson, & Corbin-Newsome, 2008). In other words, if a child is going to become a fluent speaker, she will do so, regardless of what other alternative communication systems she is introduced to. Exposing a child to an alternative system does not diminish her interest in, use of, or success in vocal communication. In fact, it may facilitate vocal language development.

In addition, providing a child with an effective means of communication has many other very significant positive effects. Perhaps most importantly, it can reduce challenging behaviors. Once the child can express her needs and wants, her frustration is drastically diminished. The child is able to influence her environment and can gain access to preferred items and activities (e.g., Ganz & Simpson, 2004; Ganz, Simpson, & Corbin-Newsome, 2008). This has been impressively demonstrated in studies using the Picture Exchange Communication system (PECS) (e.g., Anderson, Moore, & Bourne, 2007; Charlop-Christy et al., 2002; Frea, Arnold, & Vittimberga, 2001).

PECS has also been associated with increases in other social/communicative behaviors such as eye contact and joint attention skills. These are substantial advantages, given the behavioral and social difficulties associated with autism. Research clearly shows that the use of PECS improves these core symptoms of autism, in addition to teaching effective communication skills.

The fears about introducing systems are indeed unfounded, and most families are quite relieved to hear that using an alternative system will not impede their child's speech. However, it can still be a challenge to decide whether to pursue sign language or PECS. Families may hear conflicting advice from professionals with different opinions and preferences.

The Picture Exchange Communication System

The Picture Exchange Communication System (PECS) was developed by Andy Bondy and Lori Frost to address the social and communicative deficits of individuals on the autism spectrum (Bondy & Frost, 1994). It requires that the person using the system communicate with a conversational partner, a listener. Thus, the individual with autism is taught that communication must take place with another person.

As the name suggests, the system involves giving pictures to a partner in order to communicate. The pictures can be actual photos or drawings of items and concepts. The pictures are mounted on a card and laminated. In early stages of training, the child with autism is prompted to pick up a picture of something she enjoys doing or having (such as swinging or chips) and to hand it to a communicative partner by reaching toward him or her and releasing the picture in the partner's hand. The partner immediately reinforces the child for communicating her wishes by giving her what is on the card. In later stages, the child learns to walk across a distance to the communicative partner, put two or more cards together in a sentence strip to express more complex ideas, and to carry around the PECS books with all her words in them so she can communicate wherever she goes.

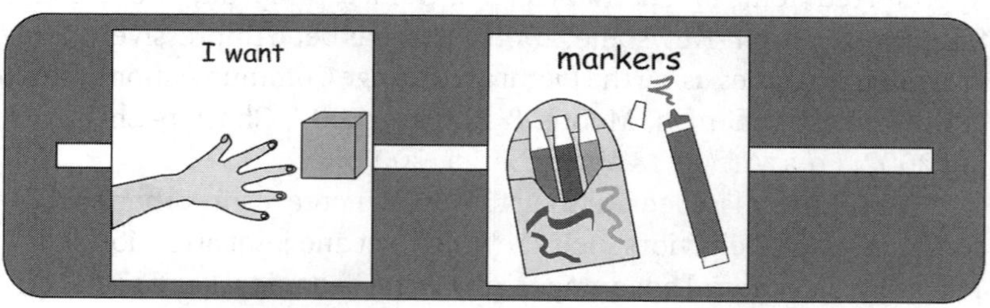

PECS is based on Skinner's analysis of verbal behavior, and focuses tremendously on manding, especially in the early phases of instruction. Children are taught to find a listener and to communicate with a listener. Persistence skills are built into the training protocol, so that the child travels to a listener and persists in communicating until the message has been received.

Perhaps the greatest advantage of PECS is that it is universally understood by listeners. No special training is required of the listener since the pictures are clearly recognizable and later are often labeled with a word. In addition, there is no need for a translator, as independent communications are understood by members of the broader community.

The major disadvantage of PECS is the reliance on equipment. The individual is at a loss to communicate if the equipment (individual picture cards or communication book) is unavailable. Furthermore, there may be some locations in which it is impossible to communicate via PECS (such as in a swimming pool). Communication at these times can become quite challenging. Another disadvantage is that it can be time-consuming for children to locate the picture, construct the sentence, and make the exchange. All of these components reduce the efficiency of the communication and build in a delay until the child's need(s) can be met.

To summarize, PECS is easy to teach and readily understood by others. Most individuals who communicate with PECS can be quite independent in its use, and do not require additional support or translation. However, the system requires equipment and is less time-efficient than vocal or sign communication.

More data are accumulating about PECS, and we can more confidently make statements about its effectiveness as a communication system, as well as about improvement in areas such as eye contact, and joint attention associated with its use (e.g., Tincani, 2004). At this point, the data on PECS are much more substantial than data available on using sign language to communicate (e.g., Schwartz & Nye, 2006).

Sign Language

Many of the professionals who use the verbal behavior classification system in an AVB model recommend sign language for children with autism who are not yet using speech to communicate (e.g., Sundberg & Partington, 1999; Partington & Sundberg, 1998). These professionals generally point out several advantages of sign, including the fact that it's constantly available as a mode of communication. That is, people always have their hands with them, while they may not have a PECS book with them. They also point out that sign language tends to be efficient. Responses are made very quickly, and communication can be rather immediate. This may be an especially important advantage when any delay in communication may increase the child's frustration and challenging behaviors.

Advocates of sign also point out that there is a community of people who speak with sign—the deaf community. (In our experience, most children with autism in the U.S. are taught to use American Sign Language, the same sign language system used by the majority of deaf sign language users.) PECS users cannot find a similar community. Finally, advocates often point out some theoretical advantages of sign language. They view sign as more analogous to vocal speech, because each sign is made distinctly, just as each word is distinct from all other words. PECS, on the other hand, involves an identical response regardless of what is being communicated. That is, the person always scans the available pictures, selects her choice, and then communicates that choice to a conversational partner. For this reason, PECS is referred to as a selection-based communication system. (This is in contrast to a topographical system, such as vocal speech or sign, in which every single item is uniquely created. The hands or mouth are configured in different ways to communicate many different things.)

It is difficult to argue with these points. It is true, for example, that many deaf people communicate with sign. It is also true that PECS is a selection-based system of communication. Whether these facts actually make sign a better communication system choice, however, is not clear.

In addition, many professionals point out some potential disadvantages to sign language. Perhaps the most commonly cited objection to it is that very few people understand sign language. It is quite unlikely that people who are not deaf will understand signed communication. This necessitates the presence of a translator, which significantly reduces the potential for complete independence of the person with autism. While someone could order independently at McDonald's with a picture communication system, they cannot do so via sign language.

Furthermore, many individuals with autism have significant motor difficulties. Often children with autism use signs that are highly idiosyncratic, and that will not be readily understood, even by those who know sign language. This further increases their dependence on others to help them get their wants and needs known.

There are some additional theoretical and clinical arguments that advocates of sign language point out. For example, individuals may be able to transfer sign more efficiently to other verbal operants (such as tacting, or commenting) once they have learned to mand (make requests), although research still needs to be done to prove or disprove this. In some contexts, sign may be more efficient, as more immediacy in communication is possible. So, it may be useful to teach children some sign responses, especially to allow them to communicate frustration or the need for a break.

In summary, sign language offers the advantages of efficiency and portability. It also may be more similar to vocal speech in its essential characteristics (compared to picture-based systems) and increase the efficiency of responses. However, the lack of comprehension by the

Is Sign Language Right for Your Child?

While it's true that there have been more studies on the effectiveness of PECS for children with autism than on the effectiveness of sign, the main emphasis in communication modality is matching the learner to the system. During the years in which sign fell into disfavor, it was rarely even considered for children with ASD—even for those who may have been able to use signs effectively and efficiently. One of the main advantages of the VB approach is that it has refocused the field on sign as a main communication modality choice.

For many individuals, sign may be the *best* choice. Perhaps most importantly, sign can be the *preferred* modality for many children. Children who respond well to sign use it spontaneously and will demonstrate a strong preference for it. Some learners prefer sign because they can respond more quickly and with less effort when they use it. They may find signing considerably more efficient than PECS.

In addition, some children are simply better at making sign responses vs. using a picture-based system. Sign language may be a better match than picture-based systems for children who have poor matching skills but good imitative skills. It is important for clinicians to be open to all options, and to match the student's characteristics with the system that best supports him or her.

Currently, it is common to encounter "either-or" thinking when making decisions about communication modality. That is, some clinicians may automatically recommend one modality over another. Such decisions should never be ideological, however, and should not reflect clinician preference or orientation. The decision as to what modality any given child should use should always be based on the individual learner's strengths, needs, and preferences.

broader community limits a user's independence and requires the presence of a translator. Furthermore, special training is required for others to understand signed communication.

Matching the Child and the Communication System

Over the past few years, strong opinions have been expressed about the pros and cons of sign language, PECS, and other alternative

communication methods, fueling consumer confusion. Many parents worry that they may select the wrong system.

When choosing a system for a particular child, it is important for parents and professionals alike to stay focused on that child as an individual. We need to select a system that appears to be a good match for the individual, and we need to evaluate how well it is working for her on a continual basis.

It would be helpful if we knew more about the characteristics of learners that make certain kinds of systems better choices for them. Mark Sundberg and James Partington (1998) suggested that children who imitate well may be good candidates for sign language, while children who have strengths in matching might be good candidates for a picture system. This is logical; a good imitator should be able to make comprehensible (and less idiosyncratic) signs. Similarly, a good matcher should be able to easily scan and select from an array of pictures.

It is likely that more studies on the use of sign will be done in the years to come, but currently there are few studies of sign language and autism. Once additional research has been completed, we will hopefully develop more empirically derived (data-based) guidelines for making decisions regarding communication modality.

Making Individualized Choices

It may be helpful to avoid thinking you must select one communication modality for your child and use that exclusively. Instead, you may wish to try a ***total communication*** approach, which speech-language pathologists have been advocating for many years. In this model, all modalities of communication are explored. The child is taught signs, exposed to pictures, and encouraged to vocalize. Over time, the child's preferences emerge and her strengths become more evident. Our skills in data collection can be used to help identify these preferences and strengths, leading to a highly individualized decision for that child.

If you are trying to decide on a communication modality for your student or child, here are some questions you should consider:

1. Has your child been assessed to understand her motor (and specifically fine motor) strengths and weaknesses? Is she a good imitator? Can she use her hands and fingers in imitation? To play with toys? To pick up small items?
2. Can your child match objects to objects, pictures to objects, and objects to pictures? Is your child good at scanning for one particular item among many?
3. If sign language is chosen for your child, will the people who will be communicating with her be able to understand and respond to your child's signs? Are family members such as siblings, aunts, and grandparents willing to learn and respond to your child's signs? Will sign be supported at school? Does your child's teacher understand sign? What about her OT, gym teacher, lunch aide?
4. If PECS is chosen for your child, will family members, including siblings, be able to use PECS with your child? Will you be willing to travel with a PECS book to the supermarket, movie theater, playground?

One good outcome of all this debate about modalities is that clinicians and parents are thinking more about a variety of ways to improve communication in children with autism. Sign language had fallen out of favor in autism intervention, and was often not considered even for children who might have benefitted substantially from it. The debate has forced us to think more systematically about all of the options, and has reemphasized the importance of matching the intervention to the individual child. We need to ensure that we do not adopt a one-size-fits-all model, and truly require assessment and monitoring of progress at the individual level.

For parents, this means that you should be regularly asked how your child's communication skills are progressing at home and you should be asked to keep data on your child's progress. Perhaps the most important thing you might be asked to track as a parent is your child's use of the communication system she is learning to use:

- How functional is it for her?
- Is she actually using it when she needs it?
- Has the system been given a fair shot? That is, did everyone involved implement the system systematically, consistently, and reliably to make a fair determination of its efficacy?

Sometimes communication modalities are abandoned early without a fair trial (without data to back up the discontinuation), perhaps because the system simply was not used enough.

Finally, be aware that your child or student should never lose communication skills because of someone else's theoretical or clinical preference for a specific modality. If your child is adept at PECS, sign language, or any other communication method, any change in communication modality should be approached with great caution. For example, a child's ability to communicate via PECS should not be taken away while she is learning to use sign. Similarly, the team should not avoid signed communication while training the child to communicate via PECS. It is unethical to remove skills or to prevent an individual from using acquired skills that are socially important.

The most important take-home messages from this discussion are:

- Providing an alternative communication system will not reduce the likelihood that a child will develop vocal speech.
- The decision as to which modality to pursue should be individualized.
- Different communication systems may be tried with a child, and her preferences and strengths can be evaluated over time.
- Data on PECS are impressive and are growing.
- It is essential that we remain focused on the individual child and make decisions based on that child's needs and progress.

References

Anderson, A., Moore, D. & Bourne, T. (2007). Functional communication and other concomitant behavior change following PECS training: A case study. *Behaviour Change, 24,* 1–8.

Barbera, M. & Rasmussen, T. (2007). *The Verbal Behavior Approach: How to Teach Children with Autism and Related Disorders.* New York, NY: Jessica Kingsley Publishers.

Bryson, S. E. (1996). Epidemiology of autism. *Journal of Autism and Developmental Disorders, 26,* 165-67.

Bryson, S. E., Rogers, S. J. & Fombonne, E. (2003). Autism spectrum disorders: Early detection, education, and intervention. *Canadian Journal of Psychiatry, 48,* 506-16.

Charlop-Christy, M.H., Carpenter, M., Le, L., LeBlanc, L., & Kelley, K. (2002). Using the Picture Exchange Communication System (PECS) with children with autism: Assessment of PECS acquisition, speech, social-communicative behavior, and problem behaviors. *Journal of Applied Behavior Analysis, 35,* 213-31.

Frea, W., Arnold, C. & Vittimberga, G. (2001). A demonstration of the effects of augmentative communication on the extreme aggressive behavior of a child with autism within an integrated preschool setting. *Journal of Positive Behavior Intervention, 3,* 194-98.

Ganz, J. & Simpson, R. (2004). Effects on communicative requesting and speech development of the Picture Exchange Communication System in children with characteristics of autism. *Journal of Autism and Developmental Disabilities, 34,* 395-409.

Ganz, J., Simpson, R. & Corbin-Newsome, J. (2008). The impact of the Picture Exchange Communication System on requesting and speech development in preschoolers with autism spectrum disorders and similar characteristics. *Research in Autism Spectrum Disorders, 2,* 157–69.

Hall, G. A. & Sundberg, M. L. (1987). Teaching mands by manipulating conditioned establishing operations. *The Analysis of Verbal Behavior, 5,* 41-53.

Lamarre, J. & Holland, J. G. (1985). The functional independence of mands and tacts. *Journal of the Experimental Analysis of Behavior, 43,* 5-19.

Lord, C. & Paul, R. (1997). Language and communication in autism. In F. R. Volkmar & D. J. Cohen (Eds.) *Handbook of Autism and Pervasive Developmental Disorders.* 2nd ed. Hoboken, NJ: John Wiley & Sons.

Michael, J. (1982). Distinguishing between discriminative and motivational functions of stimuli. *Journal of the Experimental Analysis of Behavior, 37,* 149-55.

Partington, J. W. & Sundberg, M. L. (1998). *Assessment of Basic Language and Learning Skills (The ABLLS): An Assessment for Language Delayed Students.* Pleasant Hill, CA: Behavior Analysts, Inc.

Schwartz, J. & Nye, C. (2006). Improving Communication for Children with Autism: Does Sign Language Work? *Evidence Based Practice Briefs, 1,* 1-17.

Skinner, B. F. (1957). *Verbal Behavior.* Acton, MA: Copley Publishing Group.

Sundberg, M. L. (2004). A behavioral analysis of motivation and its relation to mand training. In L. W. Williams (Ed.) *Developmental Disabilities: Etiology, Assessment, Intervention, and Integration.* Reno, NV: Context Press.

Sundberg, M. L. (2007) A brief overview of a behavioral approach to language assessment and intervention for children with autism. *ABA: International Newsletter.*

Sundberg, M. L. & Michael, J. (2001). The value of Skinner's analysis of verbal behavior for teaching children with autism. *Behavior Modification, 25,* 698-724.

Sundberg, M. L. & Partington, J. W. (1999). The need for both discrete trial and natural environment language training for children with autism. In P. M. Ghezzi, W.L. Williams & J.E. Carr (Eds.) *Autism: Behavior Analytic Perspectives.* Reno, NV: Context Press.

Tincani, M. (2004). Comparing the Picture Exchange Communication System and sign language training for children with autism. *Focus on Autism and Other Developmental Disabilities, 19,* 152-63.

3 Emergence of Language

Imagine if you had no effective way of expressing your needs or wants. You couldn't ask for water instead of milk, you couldn't ask to have the TV volume turned down, and you couldn't ask for help reaching something from a high shelf. It would be pretty frustrating, wouldn't it? That is why young children with autism spectrum disorders need to learn to mand—ask for what they need and want. In ABA programs, manding is usually the first verbal behavior that is worked on.

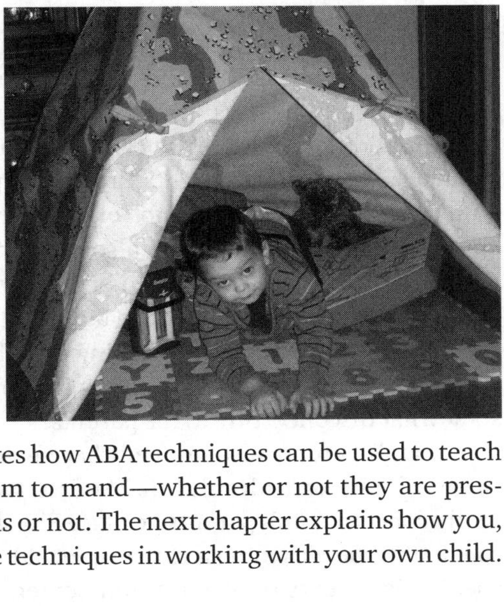

This chapter illustrates how ABA techniques can be used to teach young children with autism to mand—whether or not they are presently making verbal sounds or not. The next chapter explains how you, the parent, can apply these techniques in working with your own child.

Sam's Early Developmental Difficulties

Sam was born a healthy baby. His parents had an older son, Ray, who was just turning two when Sam was born. As an infant, Sam was quiet and alert. He was easy. He slept, ate, and mouthed toys. Nothing seemed out of the ordinary, until he was about 12 months of age. At 12 months, Sam began overreacting to many sensations. For example, he appeared to have a heightened sense of touch and an intense focus with his vision. He would arch his back when hugged and would stop and stare at ceiling fans, light coming through the window, and cars passing by outside in the street. Still, Sam was mastering many skills on schedule, learning to crawl, cruise, and then walk at 15 months of age. He sometimes liked to feed himself and was interested in toys, especially toys that spun.

When he was about one, Sam had very specific interests and found ways to entertain those interests. A favorite pastime was opening and closing cupboard doors. Since Sam couldn't reach the cupboards himself, he would cry to be picked up or would stand by the cupboards and reach his arms up to his parents until they picked him up and let him touch the shiny knobs. Like other children, Sam liked to repeat his actions and to explore how things worked and he was persistent about his explorations.

Although Sam did many things other typically developing children do when they explore, his parents noticed that his interests were restricted. Besides opening the cupboard doors, he also liked opening and closing room doors, sliding doors, microwave doors, and cabinets. When Sam's parents tired of helping him play with doors, Sam didn't seem to accept "no" or understand that the opening and closing "game" was over. Sam also liked things that spun, especially the washing machine. He would become excited and run toward the laundry room whenever he heard Mom and Dad open the door or start the machine. Watching the clothing tumble was fascinating to Sam. Watching Sam stare at the machine for an entire cycle, though, was somewhat disconcerting to his parents.

Sam's parents also noticed that he was not babbling or saying "mama," "up," or "yah yah yah." At first, this particular delay did not really concern Sam's parents because Ray, Sam's older brother, didn't speak until he was almost three years old. Now that Ray was able to speak, his parents frequently commented on how hard it was to get him to be quiet! They assumed that Sam would be a late talker too, just like his big brother. Sam's parents did not jump to any conclusions. They decided to monitor Sam's development.

As the days and weeks passed, Sam's mom grew increasingly concerned about his development. She felt it in her gut; something was not right. It was not just Sam's late start on speech, but also his unusual way of interacting. He didn't seem to respond to her in typical ways such as running up to her as Ray had done (and continued to do) when she returned from work.

Of course, she knew all children were different, but Sam's behavior had a qualitative difference that she thought only a parent could feel. What was it? It wasn't exactly that Sam wasn't connecting with her. He could and did make eye contact, though it wasn't always consistent, and sometimes it was as though he looked through her and not at her. And he definitely connected with her when he wanted her to get him a bottle, to pick him up, or to turn on the washing machine so he could watch it spin. It wasn't that Sam didn't connect at all, but that he lacked a *meaningful, consistent,* and *reciprocal* connection. That is, Sam connected to things that mattered to him, usually inanimate objects, and not to his parents, grandparents, or older brother. With Ray, the reciprocity flowed; his parents didn't have to work at the relationship. The story was different with Sam. His mom thought it was okay that he didn't run up to her when she came home from work, but it was not okay that he didn't look, or want to be hugged, or hug back and smile.

As developmental concerns about Sam mounted, his parents took him to a scheduled 15-month appointment with his pediatrician. The pediatrician asked Sam's parents all kinds of questions, specific questions about developmental milestones, interaction, language, and play they later could not recall. What they did recall was the uneasiness with which they left the doctor's office. This concerned Sam's parents beyond description. It was so easy to understand and know what to expect when Sam had physical ailments such as ear infections and fluid build-up that could be treated with medication and ear tubes. It was also easy to understand how the treatments ameliorated the problems. In contrast, the things that were not right with Sam now were not physical, and they were harder to understand, and even harder to see clearly. Sam's parents understood that the problem Sam had was not something an antibiotic was going to fix. It was a larger problem, a problem that affected his overall functioning.

At the appointment, the pediatrician had recommended that Sam's parents contact early intervention services and obtain an evaluation. At this evaluation, Sam was found to be delayed in all areas of development, including language, gross motor, speech, and cognitive skills. These delays qualified him for early intervention services. The early intervention evaluation was the first step in beginning the process of understanding Sam, obtaining a formal diagnosis, and obtaining the appropriate services. Sam was diagnosed with an autism spectrum disorder at 26 months of age. After some research, Sam's parents were able to obtain services from an agency specializing in the treatment of autism spectrum disorders using ABA. A number of professionals, including a speech therapist and behavior analyst, were assigned to his team.

Fostering Sam's Vocal Play

When the behavior analyst first met Sam and his parents, one of the first questions she asked was, "Does Sam make any sounds at all? Does he engage in vocal play?" Sam's parents replied that Sam could say, "da-da-de-de" and sometimes make the "s" sound. Sam usually made these sounds during song-time at the daycare. Sometimes, Sam also initiated some sounds in the form of humming a melody, as if to ask his parents, "Can you sing *Row, Row, Row Your Boat* to me?"

Sam's team thoroughly assessed his sound emissions using direct observation, an assessment tool called the ABLLS-R (Assessment of Basic Language and Learner Skills-Revised), and various developmental checklists and standardized assessments. Slowly but surely, an inventory of *any* sounds that Sam made spontaneously was established. The behavior analyst tried some sounds out with Sam too. "Say Ba." No response. "Say Ba-ba-ba-ba-ba." No response. Say "SSSSSS." No response. "Say Tee." No response. The team discovered that they did not have much *control* over Sam's sound production. He would not imitate a sound that others made on demand, even if it was a sound he made spontaneously. This would soon change with a procedure called Stimulus-Stimulus Pairing of Sounds.

The Stimulus-Stimulus Pairing Procedure

The Stimulus-Stimulus Pairing Procedure (Sundberg, Michael, Partington, & Sundberg, 1996) calls for creating an environment in which a child who uses few or no sounds hears many repetitions of the speech sounds he is able to produce paired with fun and reinforcing activities. In some cases, the child gradually learns to make these sounds on demand and spontaneously.

To use this procedure with Sam, his team and parents began by identifying the sounds he sometimes made on his own. Then the team and his parents began to identify and create a list of all kinds of toys and activities that Sam enjoyed. (This is what behavior analysts refer to as a reinforcer list. See Table 3-1 for an example). For instance, Sam loved books and being sung to. He also loved certain toys such as tops and balls, and activities such as being chased around and tickled.

Since Sam loved watching tops spin, the team decided to use tops as reinforcers and for reinforcing activities in their sessions. Professionals working with Sam took the tops, spinning them and saying, "SSSSSSpin" at each swivel. Throughout Sam's first few instructional sessions, you could hear "Sssspin!"—over and over, several times a day, as Sam smiled and watched all sorts of tops take off. Bright tops that lit up with speed, snowflake-shaped tops, swirled colored tops, tops that made music while spinning—you name it; the team had it. Sam began to welcome the sight of practitioners and therapists entering his home, for he knew that they would "Ssspin" his favorite toy and he would get to watch. For a few days, this procedure occurred during each session as data were collected on Sam's own ability to say "Ssss."

Within a few sessions, Sam began to make the "Ssss" sound whenever an adult would insert a small pause just before setting that top down to spin. She would say, "Sam, look . . . a top, I'm going to SSSSSPIN IT" as she held the top ready to wind it on the floor. Sam looked in anticipation, and began to form his lips to produce the "S" sound and sure enough a soft, but audible, "Ssss" emerged—followed by cheers and shouts of joy from instructors and parents. This seemingly small accomplishment was grand for Sam and his parents. Again, holding the top, pausing for "Ssss" from Sam and saying, "Sssspin" while letting it go, each professional working with Sam repeated the action as long as Sam was interested in the top. Sam was not only saying "Ssss" but also making eye contact with instructors while doing so. "Ssss," Sam would say.

A couple of sessions later, Sam began to say "Ssss" just upon seeing the top, as if he were requesting it when seeing it. Behavior analysts would classify this verbal behavior as a mand/tact—meaning that he was motivated to request the top after he saw it. This was a significant accomplishment for Sam, as learning had occurred. He was beginning to understand that "Sssss" could possibly be used to ask to have the top spin, and it was that easy—just say "Ssss."

Table 3-1 | Sample Reinforcer List				
Name:			**Date:**	
Gustatory (Taste)				
Chips				
Juice				
Olives				
Olfactory (Scent/Smell)				
Coffee				
Flowers				
Perfume				
Thermal (Temperature)				
Ice cube				
Water bottle				
Sitting by a heating vent				
Tactile (Touch)				
Soft cloths				
Balls (e.g., koosh)				
Vibrating toy				

Visual (Perception/Looking)				
Tops				
Ball drop games				
Visual timers				
Auditory (Sounds)				
Songs				
Books with sound				
Vestibular (Movement/Motion)				
Chasing				
Picking up in air				
Trampoline				
Social Reinforcers				
Hugs				
Kisses				
Praise				
Tickles				
Peekaboo				

Later, Sam's team members and parents were able to get him to say the /s/ sound on demand, by asking Sam to say "s" (pure vocal imitation) even in the absence of the top. As a reward, he would get to watch the top spin, hold it, or try to spin it himself.

Mand Training for Sam

At the same time that Sam was learning to vocalize sounds he was also learning to *mand* or *request* that a top be spun by saying "Sss." Immediately after being asked, "What do you want?" in the presence of the top, Sam was prompted to vocally imitate the /s/ sound. With some shaping through differential reinforcement, Sam began to respond "Sss" when the top was present and only the question "What do you want?" was asked. Sam was becoming a pro at requesting spinning the top.

The team was now thinking ahead: "What else can we have Sam request?" Based on the informal preference assessment, in which a list of reinforcing items and activities was created, it appeared as though Sam enjoyed watching bubbles vanish in the air, eating chips, drinking juice, and playing with cars. He was also motivated to be picked up by his dad, especially when he wanted to open up a cupboard door or the microwave. Sam's team observed him daily and asked questions about his routine experiences. They noted all of the contexts in which Sam was making requests, even though some of his requests were not vocal, appropriate, or functional. For example, sometimes he made requests by grabbing, running from his chair, and seeking out interests such as opening and closing the garage door.

Sam's team regarded every opportunity to request as an opportunity for him to learn. They used these requesting opportunities to plan for *mand training sessions*.

With mand training (or teaching how to request), one of the most important variables operating is motivation. When someone is motivated to obtain something, he is more likely to try to obtain the item he wants. People can be motivated for many different things: food, water, warmth, asking a question to obtain an answer, toys, video games, writing an email, taking a picture, talking to someone, etc. Motivation is constantly changing. In fact, it fluctuates depending on one's state of satiation (fullness) or deprivation. For example, if you just finished a big Thanksgiving meal, your state of hunger is probably going to be low; thus, you will not have the motivation or need to eat. However, if you just woke up from a long night's sleep, your motivation to eat might be different because you have been in a state of deprivation for several hours (fasting while sleeping). Thus, you will be motivated to obtain food to satisfy your hunger.

With Sam, it was critical for the team to identify opportunities in which his motivation to *request* was very high. They created a list of these opportunities in all contexts in which Sam was likely to be motivated to ask for items or activities. The team then developed a list of sounds or words that they believed Sam could learn to make in order to request each item or activity. This list was based on the sounds that his parents and team members had already observed him making spontaneously. These opportunities included some of the behaviors and their associated *mand(s)* as outlined in Table 3-2.

Table 3-2 | Sounds Chosen for Sam to Use as Mands

Behavior	Mand (Request)
Any time Sam wanted to be picked up by his dad (or others)	"Up"
Whenever Sam wanted the top for spinning	"Sss" for spin
Asking to have things opened—usually doors, such as cupboards, microwave doors, or doors on a toy, a lid, or box	"O" for Open
Asking to get up from his chair to run	"Up"
Wanting to go to Mom or Dad	"Mama" or "Daddy"
Requesting chips to eat	"Ch-Pah" or "Chip"
Blowing bubbles	"Bah" for Bubbles
Requesting favorite toys	"Tah" for Top "Bahsss" for Bus

Once contexts and situations to request were identified, the team actively capitalized on the natural situations that arose in which Sam was motivated to request the above items/activities by providing Sam with the items/activities he requested and by slowly shaping how he requested. For example, in the beginning, when Sam wanted some-one to sing to him, he would grab the person's hands and push them together as if asking them to roll their hands in time to "The Wheels on the Bus." Later, the team members added more criteria—reaching wasn't enough; Sam also had to look at them. Once he looked and reached, they changed the criterion again; he had to say "Bahsss" to

Reinforcement Schedules

Reinforcing the child for correct responses is a central principle in the ABA approach to teaching. In ABA, when the child is learning a new skill, reinforcement is planned and delivered for *every* correct response. Behavior analysts call this a ***continuous schedule of reinforcement.***

Later on, reinforcement is given more sparingly so that the newly learned behavior is maintained and so that reinforcement is on a more natural schedule. Behavior analysts refer to this reinforcement as ***intermittent.***

If you think about it, in real life, when we see our children do something new for the first time, we tend to provide reinforcement for every response or almost every response that we see or hear. Once the child masters the skill, we decrease our reinforcement and provide it for every few responses that we observe.

It turns out that what behavior analysts call intermittent reinforcement is quite good and emulates natural schedules of reinforcement in the real world. Intermittent schedules also provide us with some other great advantages: 1) They are easier to implement since you do not have to worry about reinforcing each and every response; 2) they promote persistent behavior that is resistant to extinction; and 3) they prevent satiation since fewer reinforcers are given.

Your child's reinforcement schedules should be specified in the teaching plan. Other terminology related to reinforcement you may see includes:

- Ratio schedules: Reinforcement is based on the number of behaviors required to receive a reward
- Interval schedules: Reinforcement occurs based on the passage of time (e.g., at five-minute intervals)
- Fixed schedules: The requirements for reinforcement are always the same or fixed in number or time
- Variable schedules: The requirements for reinforcement change randomly according to the number of responses (ratio) or amount of time passed (interval).

request the bus song. Thus, by systematically teaching Sam specific behaviors, they were able to shape functional requesting from grabbing, to reaching, to making eye contact, to saying "Bahss." Eventually, Sam reliably requested "The Wheels on the Bus" song across people and contexts, thus generalizing what he had learned in isolated teaching.

Expanding Opportunities for Mand Training

It is critical to use natural situations to work on requesting with your child, since they will provide multiple opportunities to practice. Sometimes, however, the opportunities for such situations are limited for various reasons. Additionally, we know that children on the autism spectrum require frequent opportunities to learn skills and to practice them with different people and in different settings. For example: If Sam wasn't motivated to eat after a bite or two of his chips, it was difficult to have him request a chip if he really didn't want it. Sometimes, he was done playing with a toy and would toss it aside. Other times, it wasn't practical to continue to work on only one request such as "spin."

To overcome these problems, Sam's instructors began *contriving* situations in which Sam would be motivated to request. These contrived situations are often referred to as ***manding sessions***. In Sam's case, manding sessions were held daily for about ten to fifteen minutes, two to three times per day. During these sessions, each instructor actively created opportunities to request. They did so by affecting Sam's motivation to request items or activities from the pre-established list. For example, the instructors put favorite toys such as tops into containers and Sam had to say "O" for open in order for the tops to be made available. Then the instructor would hold a top in a ready-to-spin position and "hold out" with an expectant look or use a time delay, waiting for Sam to say "Sss" for spin. As soon as he did, he was reinforced with the exact thing he requested.

To increase Sam's motivation to obtain his favorite snacks, his parents were asked to reserve the goodies and to only give him free access to them if he requested them appropriately. His parents were also advised not to provide the goodies if Sam threw a tantrum to try to obtain them. (Providing reinforcement for a tantrum is not advisable, and, in fact, can make the behavior worse.)

Manipulating the environment to create opportunities for Sam to mand served several functions. The primary purpose was to teach him how to request appropriately. However, it also taught him how to initiate and communicate with other people. Finally, it associated (or paired) instructors and learning with fun activities and desired items. These additional benefits were critical for Sam, as before the start of mand training, he appeared to be unmotivated to interact or be with others. It was also important for the instructors to experience Sam in a reinforcing context, to have opportunities to reinforce him, and to be associated with positive experiences.

Using Alternative Systems

Even though Sam was learning to make sounds to signal to his parents that he wanted certain things/activities, the team felt Sam would also benefit from learning to use an alternative system that everyone in his environment could understand.

When Sam first began ABA therapy, his language skills were assessed using the *Assessment of Basic Language and Learner Skills-Revised* (ABLLS-R), parent interview, direct observation, developmental checklists, and other standardized tools. These tests and observations showed that Sam did not have a strong and reliable mode of communication. That is, Sam could not vocalize, sign, gesture, or use pictures to communicate in an appropriate manner. The team knew that Sam would need to learn to use a system or systems of communication that would enable him to express his wants and needs in a functional and reliable manner.

As mentioned in the previous chapter, many variables are considered in choosing the best alternative communication system for a child with autism. The assessment for Sam revealed that he was a poor imitator of both vocalizations and motor movements. In addition, he often communicated primarily through maladaptive behavior—crying, banging objects, and pulling others to objects to make his needs known. Finding a mode of communication for Sam was essential to decreasing his challenging behaviors and increasing appropriate communication. This goal took precedence over all other skills to be taught.

After reviewing the assessment results, Sam's team and parents decided to teach him to use the Picture Exchange Communication System (PECS) rather than sign language to communicate. This decision was reached because:

1. Sam had poor fine motor skills and imitation skills, which would likely make it difficult for him to acquire sign language.
2. Sam had previously spent several months trying to learn signs, but had learned only one sign—"more." It had over-generalized, and he used it as the sign for everything he wanted.
3. Sam's parents were willing to implement and use PECS throughout the day

As discussed in Chapter 2, Sam's parents, like many parents, wondered, "Will our child use PECS as a *crutch* for speaking?" They also worried that Sam would become *dependent* on always having to use pictures to communicate. Both of these concerns turned out to be unfounded. Once Sam learned how to communicate with PECS, his challenging behaviors such as screaming and crying decreased. Both he and his parents experienced much less frustration once he was able to use PECS to effectively communicate his needs. In addition, Sam gained some functional words as a result of PECS. Sam's team often refers to PECS as Sam's *voice* which is always carried with him.

Jason's Route to PECS

In Sam's case, both his team and his parents agreed on a communication method early in his education. Fortunately, the method selected for him, PECS, turned out to be the right system for him, and Sam almost immediately began to make steady progress in communication skills. Sometimes, however, families and teams disagree on a communication system, or the first communication system chosen for a child does not work out. What happens then? Jason's story illustrates how team members and parents can work together for the best outcome when a child's communication system is not effective.

Unlike Sam, Jason was a first child and it was apparent to his parents from very early in infancy that something was off with his development. He was slow to sit up, crawl, use his hands, and walk. Jason was also a fussy baby who cried often and was difficult to console. He had difficulty with feeding and appeared not to like being touched or cuddled. Jason's eye contact was odd and he rarely babbled. He was, however, intensely interested in books and electronic toys. He could sit for long periods, flipping through books. Like Sam, Jason had difficulty making his needs known. He often cried or had tantrums when he wanted something. Jason also had a peculiar way of observing things, studying items from his periphery (from the sides of his eyes) and sometimes spinning and looking at objects in the same manner.

Jason was almost three when his ABA team began working with him. Prior to that, he had been in an early intervention program in another state. Before we even met Jason, his parents informed us that he was a "signer" and had several signs in his repertoire which he used with prompting. When we first assessed Jason, it was clear that he was an early learner—meaning he still required a lot of skill building and support to communicate effectively.

Jason's team worked with him for weeks on various areas of skill development, including manding (making requests with sign language). When it was time for the first team meeting to discuss Jason's progress, many of the instructors expressed concern that he was not progressing with sign language. In fact, several instructors were not even sure which signs Jason was and was not able to make. Based on data on the current work that was being done with Jason as well as the assessments that had been completed, the team recommended that Jason switch to PECS instead.

Initially, Jason's parents refused to introduce PECS, arguing that signing was working for their son. The team agreed that they would continue to track Jason's acquisition of signs and the amount of prompting used over the coming weeks and then reconvene to consider other communicative options. As the days passed, it became more apparent to Jason's parents that their son was dependent on prompts to use his signs and also tended to scroll through many signs as if searching for the correct one to use. This caused Jason to inadvertently practice errors. Most importantly, Jason's signs had been modified so much—because of his fine motor and gross motor difficulties—that they were only understood by people who knew him very well; namely, his parents and instructors who worked closely with him. This was a concern for the team and his parents as they envisioned long-term difficulties in school and other settings where Jason's unique signs would not be understood by others.

Jason's parents requested literature on PECS, signing, and communication alternatives, and then made an informed decision based on

Jason's data and the scientific literature. With some trepidation, they agreed to try PECS. However, Jason's team and parents also agreed that if Jason used an appropriate sign to communicate, it would be reinforced. Thus, Jason would not be discouraged from using any appropriate signs he knew, and would also learn how to communicate using a new system—one that turned out to require less effort from Jason.

It is important to highlight how critically important it was for Jason, as well as for his team, to acknowledge and reinforce any appropriate communication attempt. It is also important to note that PECS was agreed upon as a communication system based on assessment and objective facts related to Jason's skills rather than on a preference (one way or another) by either the team or parents. Sometimes these types of issues present ethical dilemmas if there is a feeling that once a new communication modality is chosen, the old communication modality should not be reinforced. It would be unethical not to reinforce a child's appropriate attempts to communicate, however. Every effort to teach the best approximations should be made as more functional skills are taught. The decision as to what communication modality to use and reinforce should always be learner-driven, and all communication attempts—no matter the modality—should be reinforced.

Jason's Early PECS Training

When Jason began using PECS, the team began with manding sessions. First they identified a variety of reinforcers—items that Jason was highly motivated to work for, including salty chips, puzzles he enjoyed doing, and pictures he liked to look at. The team took numerous pictures of Jason's reinforcers, printed and laminated them, and applied Velcro to them to use in his PECS book.

Two people were needed to begin Jason's PECS training. One person (the prompter) sat behind Jason, ready to prompt him to reach for his PEC icon whenever he wanted a chip and then approach another person, the ***communicative partner,*** to exchange the picture for a chip. As long as Jason's motivation was high for chips, the team kept working with him. By the end of the training session, Jason had acquired the response of *reach, pick up, and exchange* an icon to request his salty chips! The team was hopeful and his parents were elated.

With some practice with different people and with a variety of reinforcers, Jason was able to quickly move into phase II of PECS, in which he worked on *distance* (walking across a room to either pick up an icon or taking an icon to someone across a room) and *persistence* (trying over and over until you get what you want or your "message" is heard). Phase II was a critical learning period for Jason, as it emphasized the importance of generalizing the skills from Phase I to different environments, people, and stimuli. Another reason Phase II is important is that it continues to be used throughout PECS training (even in later phases), as the PECS user will always need to persist, travel, and request in novel environments.

Within a short week, Jason quickly moved from Phase II of PECS to Phase III. In Phase III, Jason learned to discriminate between the pictures of preferred and nonpreferred items and to use the appropriate picture to request the item he wanted. He also learned to choose between photos of two preferred items to request the one he wanted most. Jason's well-developed visual and scanning skills as well as amazing achievement in earlier phases of PECS continued as he progressed through the later phases of PECS. Jason kept using PECS as his primary communication method as he moved on to kindergarten—where he was successful in communicating with his teachers as well as his peers.

What Does Research Say about PECS?

As we mentioned in Chapter 2, there is evidence to suggest that the use of an alternative system of communication may actually help with speech and language skills. The reasons that PECS in particular may improve a child's language and speech skills are that:

1. Alternative systems provide a way for a child to communicate effectively, thereby reducing frustration associated with speech production.
2. Learning to use an alternative communication system provides the child with functional communication. Speech can be practiced (but is not required) for communication. This can reduce the demand for vocal speech, which can be especially helpful when such demands have been associated with negative behaviors.

One study that can be reassuring for parents of young children with autism to learn about was conducted by Dr. Marjorie Charlop-Christy and colleagues (Charlop-Christy et al., 2002). In this study,

three students with autism were monitored to see how long it took them to master PECS phases as well as to see what effects the PECS training had on several social-communicative behaviors. This study demonstrated that PECS actually helped to increase spontaneous and imitative speech, reduce problematic behaviors (such as tantrums and disruptions), and increase social-communicative behaviors (such as approaching and looking at others). Also impressive was the information on the efficiency of instruction. On average, it took each child approximately 170 minutes or 246 total trials to learn each phase of PECS.

Both Jason's and Sam's parents read about the study by Charlop-Christy and colleagues and found that it helped alleviate some of their fears that PECS might hinder their children's communication and acquisition of speech skills. Jason's mother later shared with the team that her fears and misconceptions of how PECS works prevented her from seeing the true strengths and weaknesses in her son's communication abilities. She admitted that until she read some of the scientific literature on PECS and sign language, she was unsure of how to proceed with Jason, simply based on lack of information.

The importance of being open to trying alternative communication systems that match the child's strengths and skills cannot be overstated. If you, as a parent, are trying to decide whether to pursue alternative communication for your child, you may want to read *A Picture's Worth: PECS and Other Visual Communication Strategies in Autism* by Andy Bondy and Lori Frost, as well as the research article by Dr. Vincent Carbone and colleagues listed in the References at the end of this chapter.

Do's and Don'ts when Using an Alternative Communication System with Your Child

Do's:

- Do think of the alternative communication system (ACS) as your child's voice and remember that your voice should travel with you wherever you go. This is easy for sign language, but you have to remember if you are using PECS.
- Do make sure that friends and family understand your child's ACS and will know how to respond to your child. This also includes siblings.
- Do consult with your child's behavior analyst when beginning training. If you decide on PECS, train faithfully and according to protocol.
- Do take data on the effectiveness of the ACS system.
- Do make decisions that are objective about the use and viability of an ACS for your child

Don'ts

- Don't anticipate what your child is trying to communicate. Wait for him to finish his request response before reinforcing him.
- Don't give up on requiring your child to use his ACS (one or two days is not enough time to test this out).
- Don't compare your child to another child with ASD. Everyone is different and needs an individualized approach to learn.
- Don't give up!

References

Bondy, A. & Frost, L. (2011). *A Picture's Worth: PECS and Other Visual Communication Strategies in Autism.* 2nd ed. Bethesda, MD: Woodbine House.

Carbone, V.A., Lewis, L., Sweeney-Kerwin, E.J., Dixon, J., Louden, R. & Quinn, S. (2006). A comparison of two approaches for teaching VB functions: Total Communication vs. vocal-alone. *Journal of Speech Language Pathology and Applied Behavior Analysis 1,* 181-92.

Charlop-Christy, M.H., Carpenter, M., Le, L., LeBlanc, L.A. & Kellet, K. (2002). Using the Picture Exchange Communication System (PECS) with children with autism: Social-communicative behavior, and problem behavior. *Journal of Applied Behavior Analysis 35,* 213-31.

Frost, L.A. & Bondy, A.S. (1994). *The Picture Exchange Communication System Training Manual.* Cherry Hill, NJ: Pyramid Educational Consultants.

Sundberg, M.L., Michael, J., Partington, J.W., & Sundberg, C.A. (1996). The role of automatic reinforcement in early language acquisition. *The Analysis of Verbal Behavior 13,* 21-37.

4 Building Language

The previous chapter provided an overview of how ABA techniques can help young children with autism learn that they can use communication skills to get their needs and wants met. This chapter expands on that information with practical strategies that can be used to teach children to make requests (mand). It also covers two other expressive language skills—tacting and echoics—that young typically developing children usually pick up automatically, but that are often problematic for children with autism spectrum disorders. Finally, the chapter provides some guidance on helping children improve their receptive language, or listening, skills.

Using Language to Make Requests (Manding)

Typically developing children learn to make requests very early in life and in many different activities and contexts. Children ask for activities that involve repeated actions and motions, funny faces and tickles, pushes on a swing and throwing a ball—the list goes on. Children also request (mand for) items that are present or absent and activities that are ongoing or absent. They make those requests of a variety of people in a variety of different ways. Take, for example, a typically developing child who is able to ask for a tickle from numerous people, in numerous settings, and at different times.

Children with autism spectrum disorders also need to learn to make requests in many different settings, with different people, and in different ways. Unlike typically developing children, though, they often do not learn how to do this on their own without a great deal of practice. That is why in ABA programs, you will see specific goals and instruction related to helping the child mand (make requests) in many different settings.

We have found that the *Verbal Behavior Milestones Assessment and Placement Program* (VB MAPP) developed by Dr. Mark Sundberg (2008) is a useful tool in helping to figure out the level of manding (or other verbal behaviors) that a child is ready to learn. It provides a behaviorally based language assessment appropriate for all children with language delays. (By "behaviorally based" we mean that the person administering the assessment observes the child's behavior during specific situations, some of which are set up to see how she will communicate/behave.) It is a particularly useful assessment because it has been field tested with typically developing children, and therefore provides a point of developmental reference regarding language.

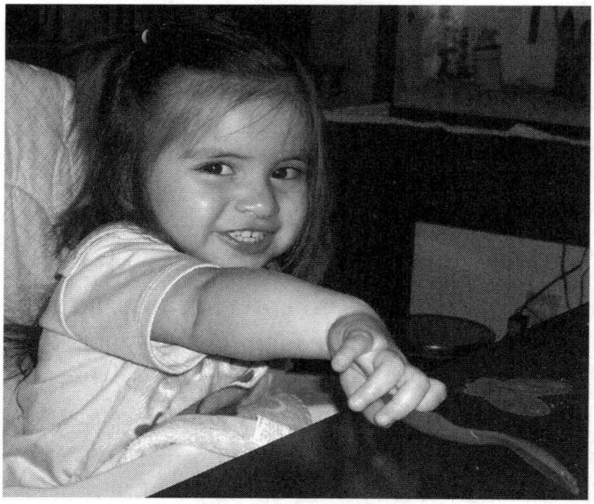

If your child's team does not use the VB MAPP to assess your child's language skills, they may use the ABLLS or ABLLS-R or one of the other assessment tools discussed in Chapter 1 in the section on "Assessing Speech and Language Difficulties."

Early Manding Skills

Understanding the developmental sequence of manding is very important because it will help you target requesting skills that are developmentally appropriate for your child and build a requesting repertoire without major "holes" in it.

It is well established that manding is one of the first forms of communication that infants develop, and that it may take on many forms. For example, an infant may cry because she wants to eat, and a two-and-a-half-year-old toddler may cry because she wants attention. These early mands (requests) are aimed at getting something that is immediately reinforcing to the child when she receives it. They are requests for objects or actions that will satisfy an immediate need or want. As children develop, mands also include requests for information (Who, What, Where, etc.), requests for complex actions ("Can you help me reach my lunchbox; it's on top of my cubby?"), requests for attention ("Look, I drew a dinosaur!"), and requests to remove aversive stimuli ("Stop stepping on my foot!").

When we think about requesting or manding skills, it is important to consider the different qualities that a mand can have, as well as the form of the mand, the context in which manding occurs, and the developmental progression of manding that occurs with typically developing children. For example, a child with autism should first be able to request a variety of items that are present throughout the day before she is expected to request objects that are out of view, actions, or information.

Determining Whether a Child Can Use Speech to Mand: Echoics

Repeating what someone just said is what behavior analysts call an ***echoic.*** It involves a direct correspondence with what was said to what is being said. For example, if I say "Pizza" and you say "Pizza," that would be considered an echoic.

It is common for young children to repeat words, phrases, and other auditory stimuli as part of the language learning process. Repeating others' sounds and words is considered to be automatically reinforcing as well as socially reinforcing. That is, children repeat words and sounds because they find it rewarding to do so (automatic reinforcement); additionally, when children repeat words they are often reinforced by parents and caregivers (social reinforcement), thus encouraging them to build their vocabulary. For example, a parent might point out a "plane" in the sky and her child repeats "plane." The parent might say, "Yes, that's right, it is a plane," providing social reinforcement to the child for repeating the word.

Sometimes children with autism spectrum disorders echo excessively, and in that case the repetition may be called ***echolalia.*** For example, if a child were to repeat back, "Do you want cookie" or "Are you okay?" when a parent asks those questions, it would be considered echolalia. With echolalia, often the intonation is exactly as the child heard it. Bear in mind that very young typically developing children may also use echolalia as a way of learning, but they usually outgrow echolalia and it is not as pervasive as it is with autism spectrum disorders. Unusual echoing in any child should be evaluated.

Generally, it is viewed as a positive sign when children with ASD imitate spoken words and sounds simply because echoic behavior can be shaped to include various aspects of spoken language. For example, if a very young child makes some vowel and consonant sounds such as "a" in cat or "e" in eat, and "b" and "m" consonant sounds, a behavior analyst might choose to use various combinations of the above to start building the beginnings of spoken language. He or she might make a list of the different combinations of consonant-vowel sounds such as "ba," "me," "be," and "ma" and then systematically, one by one, introduce each combination for the child to repeat. Later, the child might be encouraged to add consonants to the end of the word or repeat consonant-vowel-consonant-vowel sounds, such as "mama."

Parents are often asked to help the team develop a list of the sounds their child will repeat, since family members have more opportunities to witness the sounds a child makes throughout the day and observe the different contexts where sounds are made. We highly recommend consulting with a speech and language pathologist experienced in working with children on the spectrum about very early language development and what progression to use for a particular child—particularly if you have never worked on such specific programming or issues. The Language Development table at the end of the chapter gives an idea of when children usually are able to make particular vowel and letter sounds and is a useful general guide to typical language development.

If a child with autism does not have an echoic repertoire, it is often important to build one before trying to teach her to vocally mand (make requests) or tact (label). This ensures that the child has the ability to produce sounds and words and provides the instructor with an effective prompt for more advanced language skills. That is, if you can have a child repeat a word or sound as an echoic, it will be much easier to use an echoic as a prompt to teach tacting and intraverbals. For example, if you can teach a child to echo, "Cookie," then you can prompt the answer "Cookie" when you hold up a cookie to teach, "What is this?" (prompt, "Cookie"). Later, teaching an intraverbal, "What do you want to eat?" (prompt: "Say, cookie") is also easier.

Teaching Echoics

A good place to start in teaching echoics is to observe what sounds your child spontaneously uses. Then the team can begin stimulus-stimulus pairing procedures to help her develop a repertoire of sounds she can imitate, as discussed in Chapter 3 in the case of Sam. Essentially, a stimulus-stimulus pairing procedure involves associating a previously conditioned reinforcer (something your child has learned to view as rewarding, such as watching her favorite movie or listening to her favorite music) with another stimulus such as an object, vocalization, phrase, or sound (Longano & Greer, 2006). Associating a highly reinforcing thing with something that is neutral is what we call stimulus-stimulus pairing. Once this occurs, the "neutral" item starts to take on reinforcing properties. For example, a child who may have vocalized "bah" without any functional intent learns to say "bah" to mean "bubbles" after the sound has been paired with the reinforcement of blowing bubbles when she says "bah."

If your child is able to use a sound to mand for a particular item, you can help her to make that same sound as an echoic. For example, if your child learns to say "buh" to request a ball, the sequence might go like this:

- You or an instructor holds the ball that your child wants.
- Your child says "buh" to request it and is given it.
- The instructor says, "Say "buh/ball" while your child is holding it (at which point your child may echo the sound just because she heard you say it and possibly because she sees it). This is a combination of a tact and an echoic.
- Next, the instructor might cover the ball with a blanket (but should also ensure that your child is no longer motivated to request the ball) and say, "Say buh/ball." If your child repeats the word/sound, this is a pure echoic. It is important that your child does not want the ball or see the ball because then it would be hard to tell whether she was actually "tacting" or "manding" for the ball or both!

Practicing Manding at Home

To help children with ASD learn to mand in many different situations, teachers and family members alike are asked to create situations for manding during different activities and with different people. At first, this may seem like a tedious task, but it is well worth the effort.

A good place to start when figuring out how to help your child practice making requests is to think about contexts and activities that you can create for manding opportunities. It may help to make a list of your daily routines from the time your child wakes up to the time she goes to sleep. Sometimes, because parents are so embedded in their own routines, they have trouble identifying the numerous situations and contexts that exist for manding. Making a list and reviewing your day and week will help you organize and think of all the opportunities for your child to make requests. See Table 4-1 for a list of sample activities and contexts that could provide multiple opportunities for requesting.

Table 4-1 | Manding Ideas in Daily Contexts

Daily Routine	Opportunity for Request
Morning self-help routines: toileting, bathroom, brushing teeth, dressing	Requests for specific actions: "Open" (door to bedroom, bathroom) "On" (toothpaste, lights, pants, socks) "Up" (lift child up to look in mirror) "Push" to flush toilet
Breakfast	Requests for specific food items: cereal, strawberry, juice, milk, banana, water
Play	Requests for specific toys: book, top, doll, train, car, puzzle
Activities	Request for specific actions: Swing, push, up, down, open (door), come, hug, kiss, high-five
Lunch/snack	Requests for specific food items and actions: "Open" (to get cookie, cereal, etc. out of container) "Give me" (food item) "Eat" (food item) "Drink" (juice, milk) "Cut" (sandwich, meat, fruit)

It is important to realize that not all mands are taught at once. We often recommend that parents focus on one or two mands when they first start intervention, as it can be overwhelming both to the child and parents to try to teach too much.

Another common concern parents have is: "When we are working on manding, do I have to give my child everything she asks for?" For example, "What do I do if she asks for a cookie 100 times?" or "What if I don't have any more cookies?" or "What if she just wants to keep swinging on a swing, but I have to go?" Our answer is, do what you would do for any typically developing child. Say, "No more" or "All done" after a reasonable amount of cookies or ice cream or pushes on a swing.

Note that you would also not want to deny a child a cookie, push on the swing, or ice cream because she *can't* ask for it in the most optimal way you are trying to teach her (whether using vocalizations, PECS, sign, or another method). Instead, just limit the amount of the reinforcer or time with the reinforcer the child can have. "Save" the strongest reinforcement for what you decide are optimal responses. What this boils down to is you give a little reinforcement when your child attempts a response, but more reinforcement for your child's best attempts at making the ultimate target response. This is also known as shaping a behavior through *differential reinforcement.*

Requesting Objects That Are Out of Sight: Once your child can request objects that are clearly visible, she can begin to request items that are out of sight. A strategy to teach this skill is to begin by having the item present for requesting. Next, check to see if your child will ask for the item if you just hide it behind your back. Start with a highly preferred item such as a toy or food item because your child is likely to be quite motivated to obtain the item. Gradually, progress to putting items in a container that your child cannot open on her own, allowing your child to watch the item being placed. Later, the item might be placed in the cupboard, or wherever the items are naturally found.

Requesting Actions

Once a child is able to request objects, whether or not they are in sight, actions should be introduced. Often, since actions are not long lasting, children will learn to ask for things that have a repetitive nature such as pushing, opening, swinging, peekaboo, tickles, "come here," "give me," and other such actions. Many of the action requests that

are initially taught occur in the context or routine of some other event—for example, "opening" the door to go outside or "pushing" when on a swing or a scooter. When there are naturally occurring opportunities to request, the child has many opportunities to practice and reinforce the skill.

How do you teach a child with an ASD to request actions such as push, sing, jump, chase, open, and tickle?

Create Opportunities: First, you must ensure that there are opportunities in which your child is motivated to request these activities. For example, situations that might encourage a child to ask for "push" might include swinging, sitting on a tricycle or toy car, or pushing a toy car down a ramp. To help motivate a child to request "sing," you might sing while playing a CD, stop it for three seconds and wait in anticipation for the child to request that you sing again.

Prompt: Second, once the contexts and opportunities have been created, you will use prompting procedures to initially teach your child the mand. Your prompting procedure will depend on your child's particular mode of communication. For example, if she uses signs to communicate, you may first provide an imitative and physical prompt for the sign "open." That is, you would show her the sign and then physically help her to position her hands to form it. Later, you would fade out the physical prompt and just give her an imitative prompt. Later still, you would use a time-delay procedure in which you "hold out" for your child to make the sign herself.

When you prompt your child, it allows you to obtain a response from her that can be reinforced in some way and also allows you to shape the behavior. In the example above, we walked you through a specific prompt hierarchy to teach the sign "open." If we were to use a prompt hierarchy for a vocal response, we might start with the whole word (say, "open") and then fade to a *phonemic prompt* (stating only the initial "o" as a cue), and then use a time delay. One thing to remember is that you should always be thinking about how to fade your prompts out of teaching. Otherwise, you may end up creating prompt dependency.

Practice: One key to helping your child learn to make requests is to provide many opportunities to practice. Repeating the action until she has no more motivation is a good way to practice requesting skills. For instance, in the example of "open," you could place several puzzle pieces or jelly beans in a container, creating an opportunity for your child to request "open" for all eight pieces of a puzzle or for five jelly beans.

Raise the Bar: Over time, you can help your child make more complex requests for actions. For example, you may require a longer mean length of utterance (e.g., "push me again, please") rather than a single word ("push"), especially if your child has speech skills. You may also help your child request more sophisticated actions such as "Pour some water into my cup"; "Can you squeeze the ketchup?"; and "Can I count them again?" As a parent you can help increase your child's mean length of utterance by setting the bar a little higher once she masters requesting with single words. So, if your child reliably and consistently asks for a cookie by saying, "Cookie," you can then begin *requiring* her to say "Cookie please" or "I want a cookie." This would be taught through prompting, shaping, and reinforcement strategies.

As with tangible items, requesting for actions occurs in a variety of contexts and activities. When working with children on the autism spectrum, it is critical to plan and embed multiple opportunities for such requests.

Requesting "Stop" or a Change in Activities

Many very young children with an autism spectrum disorder or any other type of language delay or disorder have difficulty communicating when they want something to end or stop. Often they display challenging behaviors if they cannot communicate that they want to stop an activity such as taking a bath, formal instruction, tickles, singing, blowing up a balloon, or a game of chase. If we can provide a child with the words or other communicative alternative needed to convey her request, much of the unwanted behavior subsides. From a behavioral perspective, this makes a lot of sense; teach someone to communicate appropriately what she wants (e.g., "Stop chasing me") and the likelihood of that message being understood is very high.

Crying and screaming (if it continues) is a maladaptive form of communication for two reasons—first, because it cannot be understood, and second, because it may become reinforced. For example, Sarah may cry because she wants *combing hair* to end. If her mother stops combing her hair and Sarah stops crying, then next time, when it is time to comb hair again and Sarah cries once more, the behavior of crying would be considered reinforced. Sarah is likely to cry because in the past crying was effective in *terminating* combing hair.

Now, imagine how many other behaviors have the potential of being reinforced! If we consider the perspective of the parent who is interacting with her crying child (a rather aversive interaction), it is understandable that anyone would want to *end* their child's crying. Because others usually respond to negative behaviors (crying, screaming, hitting, head-banging, and tantrums), it can often be initially difficult for a young child to understand that there is a faster and easier way to make requests. Functional Communication Training, below, can help your child make that connection.

Functional Communication Training

One very effective strategy in teaching children with autism to use more appropriate forms of requesting is known as Functional Communication Training or FCT (Carr & Durand, 1985). FCT involves selecting a response that has the same function as the inappropriate response and teaching the child to use that response as a replacement. Take, for example, the case of Kelly, a two-year-old girl with autism, who often screamed and cried intensely when she wanted instruction to stop and when she wanted her mother's attention.

Kelly's behavioral team had determined that the screaming typically occurred when Kelly was asked to do something such as insert a puzzle piece on a board, sit down on the chair, use a fork to eat, or clap her hands in imitation. Kelly also screamed whenever she saw her mother across the room, or when her mother sat in the same room while instruction occurred. It was apparent that Kelly's requests had several functions, including allowing her to escape from demands and getting desired attention. In the beginning, her crying lasted for several minutes at a time. Since her crying delayed other demands being placed on her, it was reinforcing to her. Often, Kelly was simply unavailable to learn because her crying went on for so long.

The team decided to teach Kelly that, rather than *cry* to communicate that she wanted to end demands, she could simply touch a card indicating "Break" (a functional alternative) and communicate her needs. So, the next time a session was held with Kelly, the team members anticipated that Kelly would cry and placed a "Break" card next to her. Initially, they fully prompted Kelly to touch the card the second they saw that she was about to cry or tantrum. As soon as Kelly touched the card, she was provided with a break.

The idea of training a new alternative response is to get the new response or behavior to occur instead of, and before, the *old* behavior. In Kelly's case, the alternative response that was taught was to touch a card. The same teaching procedure could be used (teaching the response before the maladaptive behavior occurs) for a child who is vocal. However, instead of teaching the child to touch a card, you might prompt her to say, "Break, please."

Teaching FCT to very young children can be somewhat of a challenge. Parents are often very sensitive to the cries of their children and naturally want to respond to them. Children with autism may also have very significant self-injurious or aggressive behaviors that have led to the development of maladaptive behaviors.

It is essential for parents to understand the functional relationship between maladaptive behavior (such as frequent crying) and the requests the child is making. Often parents worry that if their child learns functional alternatives to escape behaviors such as saying "No" or touching a break card, then their child will continue to say or demonstrate the alternative behavior all the time. This reasoning is similar to the fear that a child will continue to request "candy" or "bubbles" all the time, once she learns to mand. Although this reasoning is correct to some degree, please understand that the goal is not to teach "escape" behavior, but to teach an appropriate communicative alternative to request "escape" or a "break." We are replacing maladaptive behavior with adaptive behavior. As you can imagine, this is very important, and may be critical if a child has behaviors that can be harmful to herself and others.

It is also important for parents to understand that once their child learns the adaptive communicative alternative, she can also learn other behaviors such as waiting after she's communicated "No" or "Break" or

"Stop." To teach your child to wait or delay reinforcement, she might first be asked to tolerate one or two more demands, do one extra task, or simply wait 30 seconds before her request is honored. The important goal here is that your child learns to communicate adaptively and appropriately and that she becomes available to learn.

Sometimes it is not possible or in the child's best interest to stop an activity that the child is protesting. Take, for example, the child who runs away screaming whenever her diaper needs to be changed or whenever it is time for a bath. Rather than postponing or avoiding the entire routine, parents may be better off teaching their child to say "Later" or "Not now" and return to the task (or demand) in a few minutes. Parents might also give a warning notice, such as "Okay, bath time in five minutes" or "You can finish your puzzle and then I will change your diaper." Children are more likely to comply when they perceive they are in control, so giving choices is a good first start.

Understanding the Function of a Behavior

Sometimes it is not clear what a child is trying to communicate through her behavior. For example, is your child crying or hitting to escape a demand? Because she wants your attention? Or because she wants you to give her something or take her somewhere? Your understanding of the function of her behavior will guide your choice of a more appropriate request to teach her. In the case of a request for attention, it might be, "Mommy, play with me?" or, "Daddy, can I have a hug or tickle?"

It may also be reassuring for parents to know that most young children exhibit some form of challenging behavior (crying, aggressions, and tantrums) and usually these behaviors are replaced with more appropriate forms of communication and socialization.

For a child on the autism spectrum, it is particularly important to understand the function of any challenging behaviors. If you are not sure of the function of a behavior, you might want to request a functional behavior assessment. A professional (such as a behavior analyst) experienced in identifying such functions can develop a specific intervention plan. For more information about determining the functions of behavior, you may want to read *Functional Behavior Assessment for Children with Autism* (Glasberg, 2005).

When Manding Goes Awry

Children with autism and language disabilities can have manding difficulties for several reasons:

- Their motivation to request may be weak.
- There may be an atypical motivation (e.g., a child only wants a specific person to sing her favorite song, or only a certain order is acceptable when taking out small figurines to play with).
- The child's motivation may be reduced because of the effort involved in requesting.
- The child may not persist in asking for items she wants or will only ask for things that are consumable or tangible.

In such cases, it is extremely important to develop a program of instruction that will help the child learn to persist with requests and to request a wide variety of items, consumables, and actions. This generally involves the following steps:

1. **Make sure the child is motivated to mand** (make requests) for objects and activities. This may involve labor-intensive work from parents and teachers such as frequently assessing what the child is motivated by, as discussed in Chapter 3. It may also involve reserving the things and activities your child prizes most for times when you want to work on manding.
2. **Make sure the child does not have to expend too much effort to mand.** For example, she might only have to give an approximation of "cookie" rather than saying the entire word and will still earn a good portion. Also make sure that initially you are giving her enough prompts and not fading prompts too soon. This way she will be sure to achieve success and receive reinforcement.
3. **Teach the child to persist in requesting** (if you want something, you are going to keep having to ask for it). It is often a good idea to limit access to other reinforcement that may be available. The goal is to create a high level of motivation, but not require the child to use a great deal of effort to obtain reinforcement.

4. **Pair consumable items and other things the child is highly motivated to request with social aspects of requesting** such as eye contact and approaching others. For example, if your child only wants candy and the Magna Doodle, pair these desirable items with another play activity or task completion item and require your child to look at you to obtain the candy. Or, set up a situation that requires your child to request the Magna Doodle from another person or only receive reinforcement after she has talked about a picture she drew on the Magna Doodle. This step is particularly important when a child has very limited wants.

Once the above issues are addressed and the child is consistently requesting objects and activities she wants, it is usually considered safe to begin thinning the schedule of reinforcement. In the beginning, you will reinforce the child's mands continuously—every time that she makes a request. When she is reliably making requests, you can start providing reinforcement intermittently. For example, you might provide a favorite food after an average of three requests instead of after every single request.

For more information on reinforcing children with ASD, you may want to read *Incentives for Change: Motivating People with Autism Spectrum Disorders to Learn and Gain Independence* (Delmolino & Harris, 2004).

Using Language to Label (Tact)

Tacting or labeling is another important function of language. Labeling of your environment can occur with things you see, hear, taste, smell, or touch. It can be simplistic or elaborate and can combine the senses (e.g., seeing and smelling pizza). Tacting occurs when the speaker names things. Often the things we see are the first things we learn to label. We might label actions (running, singing) or attributes (big, blue) as well.

It is often easier to teach and establish stimulus control over tacting because the source of control is often a stimulus in the environment. That is, the thing that "controls" the child's response is what she sees or perceives in her environment. That means we can just prompt the child to say the label for the item. (This is in contrast to manding, where the item or action the child wants (popcorn; a trip to the park) may be controlled by motivation to obtain the item/action and is not necessarily visible.)

Typically developing children may begin to tact as young as 8 or 9 months of age. For example, a 9-month-old child may say "ba-ba" for bottle and "ma-ma" for mommy. Parents often practice this language skill with their child a great deal because it is easy to label the many objects in the environment. Often, it is relatively easy to teach labels for nouns and verbs to children with autism who have some echoic or imitative ability (signing). However, labeling becomes more difficult to teach once it progresses to more abstract concepts such as prepositions (on, off, about, in, between)and attributes (pretty, heavy, tall, brown), as well as stimuli that are not observable, such as feelings of pain and joy.

What do very young children label (tact)? A child's environment centers on daily routines such as meals, baths, and play, plus interactions with parents or siblings. Children are likely to have a lot of exposure to toys, household objects such as utensils, rugs, and appliances, labels of actions in routine contexts, and labels of their own feelings and states of being. For instance, parents often talk about the banana their child is about to eat, or include labels for attributes in their language ("The oatmeal is *hot*"; "Do you want a *red* apple?"). Parents also frequently label actions as they occur ("*Bye-bye* to grandma"; "Let's *walk* to the car"; "*Push* the button on the elevator"; "We need the key to *open* the door").

The quality and amount of language that parents use to interact with their very young (under the age of three) children has been directly linked to a child's growing vocabulary and later intellectual development (Hart & Risley, 2002). That is, the more a caregiver uses language to describe and talk about what the child is experiencing, the more elaborate the child's vocabulary becomes. For children with autism, it is important to understand that labeling can be taught using very systematic procedures.

Teaching Children with Autism to Tact

Nouns and verbs (and combinations of them) are the first tacts taught. Later the child learns to use prepositions, adverbs, and adjectives when labeling.

Tacting usually begins with learning to label concrete objects. As mentioned above, typical children often learn to label the objects and items around them that are in daily use. Children with autism should also begin here, but it may be helpful to begin this type of teaching in a discrete trial format (see Chapter 2). Using objects found in the child's daily environment is a terrific place to start, because you ensure that she will encounter those items frequently. This also helps with generalization.

When you are teaching your child to label objects, it is a good idea *not* to use items that your child is strongly motivated to obtain. Otherwise, she may mand for (request) the item rather than label it (tact). For example, if your child loves chocolate chip cookies and she says "cookie" when she notices one on the table, it can be hard to tell whether she is requesting the cookie or merely commenting that she sees a cookie. After you are sure your child has satiated on an item requested (or doesn't want it anymore), you are more likely to have success teaching her to label it.

Once your child can label objects, you can begin teaching her to label actions that are ongoing and attributes such as basic colors, quantity, and other adjectives. Next you can focus on more abstract attributes such as relational properties (e.g., the ball is *underneath* the table or Maggie is *bigger than* Daniel), as well as on how something tastes, feels, or sounds.

Highlighting a specific attribute can sometimes be the most difficult aspect of teaching because individuals with autism tend to over-select, or pay attention to certain stimuli or certain aspects of stimuli. For example, when asked, "What color is this [red block]?", a child with autism might initially err by saying, "block" rather than "red." Similarly, if you place a block on the table and ask, "Where is the block?" the child might say "block" rather than "table" or "on table." To highlight an attribute such as color for your child, you might gather several different colored blocks and show her all the colored blocks next to each other, perhaps labeling them for her, before asking, "What color is this?" Likewise, to highlight size, you might gather a number of objects that are the same but only differ in size (again highlighting "size" as the attribute to pay attention to). The idea is to home in on the attributes you want the child to attend to.

To teach a preposition such as "on," you might take a cup and three or four miniature counting bears of the same color and put them in various places in relation to the cup (one is on, one is under, one is next to, one is behind). Next, ask the child "Where is THIS bear?" while you point to the bear that is *on* the cup. Later, you will progress to trying to get her to say (or sign or otherwise produce) "on," herself, by pointing to the bear that is *on* the cup and asking where it is.

Increasing the Length of Phrases

Once a child can tact using single words (nouns and verbs), you can begin increasing the ***mean length of utterance*** (MLU)—or the average number of words (or syllables) the child uses each time she speaks. Building the mean length of utterance involves the use of tacting. Increasing the length of a child's phrases can be a challenge, but much can be accomplished if you use a systematic program of tacting to build language.

To increase the MLU of a child with autism, you often need to formally teach her how to use:

- carrier phrases (such as: "I see ____," "There's a ____," "I have ____")
- possessives ("my book"; "Sarah's book")
- conversational markers (small words that mark the flow of discourse, such as "Um," "uh," "you know," "like"), and
- adjectives and other attributes ("green," "old," "heavy," "dirty," "new," etc.)

You may need to teach each of these elements separately before you teach the child to use a full phrase.

Tacting is used to increase MLU after first ensuring that the child can reliably and effectively label various aspects of her environ-

ment (what she sees, hears, tastes, smells, and feels), including nouns, verbs, adverbs, prepositions, and attributes. It is much easier for a child to master other aspects of language such as carrier phrases once she can label many things. Think about it—it wouldn't make sense to require your child to say a phrase with a long MLU such as "That is a chocolate chip cookie" if all she can do is label a few reinforcing items using single words.

Problems with Tacting

Children with autism are susceptible to a host of problems when it comes to tacting:

Scripting: Sometimes self-stimulatory and stereotypical behaviors involving repetitive labeling interfere with the development of the tact. For example, some children may engage in ***scripting,*** or repeating words or phrases they have heard or seen on their favorite video or TV show. (See Chapter 8 for a fuller discussion of scripting and its treatment.)

Generalization Difficulties: Generalization issues may also interfere with learning new labels. For example, we once knew a child who was very good at labeling, but had over-generalized labeling vehicles to the point that whenever he saw anything with wheels, he called it a "car." This is an example of overgeneralization. To guard against over-generalizing, you want to ensure that you teach sufficient examples of nouns and verbs. So, make sure to teach that a car, pick-up truck, bus, van, tractor-trailor, and limousine are all vehicles.

Difficulties with Relational Concepts: Sometimes children with autism have trouble understanding relational components of tacts such as prepositions ("on," "under") and attributes/adjectives ("hot/cold," "heavy/light," or "clean/dirty"). Also, as discussed above, children with autism may label the physical object as opposed to its attribute or relational preposition. For example, a child may say "cup" instead of "on the table" when you ask her "Where is the cup?" As you can imagine, learning such attributes is not only complex but a true achievement, even for typically developing children.

Pronoun Confusion: Many children with autism have significant difficulties understanding perspective and correctly using pronouns such as I/you/he and my/your/his. For instance, they may speak of themselves as "you." Often, when children on the autism spectrum are first taught pronouns, confusion may develop because of the natural way in which pronouns are used. For instance, you might tell your child, "touch your nose" or "get your shoes." Then, later you may ask, "Whose shoes are these?" (expecting your child to now say "*my* shoes" when previously you were talking to her about "*your* shoes."). This automatically creates confusion because the perspectives keep changing.

Sometimes it is helpful not to use pronouns with your child in everyday language, but just in instructional sessions. It can also be helpful to use third person perspective to speak of yourself or your child ("Mommy is going to take a shower now" vs. "I am going to..." or "Michael needs to put his shoes on" instead of "You need to...."). Note that when using PECS, carrier phrases are built into the sentence strip. For example, when a child is expressing "I want," she selects a single picture that signifies "I want..." and then completes the sentence with one or more pictures expressing what she wants ("big, blue ball"). After the child exchanges the strip with her communicative partner, the partner reads it back to the child from her perspective, thus avoiding confusion.

Receptive Language

Until now we have focused on what B.F. Skinner called "speaker skills" such as the mand, tact, and echoic. Our focus now will turn to what has been traditionally viewed as receptive language, but better described by B.F. Skinner using the term "listener skills." Listener skills require what the term implies—that an individual listens to what is being said and understands what is being said.

Often, understanding is measured by the listener's behavior. For example, if someone tells a child, "Put your jacket away," we would measure her understanding of the language by observing whether she put her jacket away (possibly in a cubby or on a hook). Listener behavior can also be verbal (Sundberg, 2008). For example, some questions (e.g., "What is your name?" "Where do you live?" "Do you like to eat strawberries?") may require a verbal response ("Alex," "Connecticut," and "No") rather than a behavioral response.

Receptive language or listener behavior may also involve complex relations and understanding of abstract concepts and words that are related to functions, features, and classes of items. For example, if we ask a child to put all of her toy animals away, she needs to understand that a pig, cow, dinosaur, and tiger are all in the animal class. Similarly, if we ask her to put all the things that have wheels (feature) versus things that you eat (function) in different places, she would need to understand that things can be categorized by specific features and may also be linked by certain functions (e.g., it can be eaten, or you can brush with it, if describing a toothbrush).

Perhaps one of the most common misunderstandings we encounter is that receptive and expressive language abilities are separate, rather than interconnected. Many people do not think of language in terms of function or in terms of the different speaker (expressive language) functions such as B.F. Skinner described. The good news is that once Skinner's verbal behavior is explained and demonstrated, parents and professionals alike easily understand and acknowledge that language has functions and not just form. We have found that a simplified explanation of verbal behavior is extremely helpful to understanding the complexity of language.

Typically, listener behavior or responding begins to occur very early in infant development. One of the first signs of listener behavior that parents usually observe is that their child is *listening* or *attending*

to the speaker's voice. A very young child (under the age of 12 months) does this by orienting toward Mommy's voice and following her as she moves around a room. Other early signs of receptive understanding occur when a child responds to her own name or to different voices in a room.

Listener Skills of Children with Autism

Children with autism often have listener skills that are quite impaired from very early on. They may focus on and be more interested in objects rather than people, and they may act as if they do not hear when their name is called. And yet, they may turn to look right away if they hear another type of noise such as the theme song of their favorite television show.

In addition, children with autism often have difficulty with ***joint attention,*** which is closely linked to the development of language skills. That is, early deficits in joint attention significantly affect both receptive and expressive language development (Murray, Creaghead, Manning-Courtney, Shear, Bean, & Prendeville, 2008).

Joint attention has been defined in various ways by researchers as involving different types of skills such as pointing, showing, and coordinated looking with others (Kasari, Freeman, & Paparella, 2006). The general idea, however, is that joint attention involves two observers (e.g., mother and child) both focusing on a single object or event of interest and that an important behavior known as ***referential looking*** occurs during this interaction. Referential looking refers to the idea that a child looks or directs her attention at an object or event and then *refers* back to the parent (or other person) as if to say, "Do you see what I see?" Joint attention development is typically considered a core deficit of autism spectrum disorders, but has only recently garnered much needed attention and focus (Taylor , 2008). See Chapter 6 for information on helping children with ASD improve their joint attention skills.

Treatment for Receptive Language Difficulties

Receptive language difficulties have typically been addressed by teaching children to touch or point to pictures of items or the actual items (usually nouns). Later, they are asked to select those items or pictures so that they not only know what an apple is but also what "touch" vs. "give me" means. As their listening comprehension grows, they are asked to respond to questions that expand their understanding of vocabulary and concepts. For example, instead of "Touch apple," they might be asked, "Give me something red (or "something you eat," "a fruit," or "something that grows on a tree.")

Another way to work on receptive language with young children with autism is to have them demonstrate specific actions on command. For example, early on we teach children to "wave" or "clap hands" by physically prompting them to perform the behavior and then systematically fading our level of assistance through a predetermined prompt hierarchy.

Once the child has learned basic receptive responses, she is taught to make more complex responses. She might be asked to scan more pictures or objects or to follow a longer sequence of instructions. For example, she might be told, "Get your lunchbox and put it on the table" or "Give me the cat and the apple," when presented with an array of ten pictures. Eventually, she will be taught to demonstrate that she comprehends the words for features, functions, and classes of items.

How Can Parents Help?

You and your child's team will jointly develop goals to help your child master new listener skills and will work systematically to help her achieve them. But there are also strategies you can use during the course of daily life to make it easier for your child to understand what you are saying and to help strengthen her listening skills. They include:

- ***Make your directions or commands as simple and as clear as possible.*** Use as few words as possible and do not string two or more instructions together. It may also be helpful to not use many pronouns at first. For example, say, "Follow Dad" instead of "Follow me."

- Try to ***highlight the most important information*** you need your child to attend to in your words. For example, you might speak a single word louder than the rest: "Give mommy the PINK cup."
- In your daily routine, try to ***incorporate the same kinds of prompts that are used in ABA teaching.*** For example, if you ask your child to pass her brother a napkin at the table, you might move the napkins close to her while moving other things on the table farther away. This is known as a positional prompt.
- ***Label your child's correct behavior when she responds correctly*** to spoken directions. For example, you say, "Get your shoes." After your daughter gets her shoes, say, "Awesome! You got your SHOES."
- ***Help your child learn that positive things will happen if she responds when you call her name.*** For example, say your child's name when she spontaneously provides eye contact and provide reinforcement at the same time, so that her name is *paired* with reinforcement.
- ***Avoid calling your child's name if you are only going to make a demand or reprimand her.***
- ***If your child is "tuning you out," look for novel reinforcers*** to entice her so that she will attend to you when you speak. For example, wave a highly reinforcing item in front of your child to capture her attention or begin to sing a favorite tune and stop when you have her attention. If your child is overly preoccupied with an object or toy, think of ways that you can manipulate the object to get your child's attention. For example, pretend that the Woody doll is singing a song or drinking from a cup.

Table 4-2 | Language Development	
What Should My Child Be Able to Do? Birth to One Year	
Hearing and Understanding	**Talking**
Birth–3 Months ■ Startles to loud sounds ■ Quiets or smiles when spoken to ■ Seems to recognize your voice and quiets if crying ■ Increases or decreases sucking behavior in response to sound	***Birth–3 Months*** ■ Makes pleasure sounds (cooing, gooing) ■ Cries differently for different needs ■ Smiles when sees you
4–6 Months ■ Moves eyes in direction of sounds ■ Responds to changes in tone of your voice ■ Notices toys that make sounds ■ Pays attention to music	***4–6 Months*** ■ Babbling sounds more speech-like with many different sounds, including *p, b,* and *m* ■ Chuckles and laughs ■ Vocalizes excitement and displeasure ■ Makes gurgling sounds when left alone and when playing with you
7 Months–1 Year ■ Enjoys games like peekaboo and pat-a-cake ■ Turns and looks in direction of sounds ■ Listens when spoken to ■ Recognizes words for common items like "cup," "shoe," "book," or "juice" ■ Begins to respond to requests (e.g., "Come here" or "Want more?")	***7 Months–1 Year*** ■ Babbling has both long and short groups of sounds such as "tata upup bibibibi" ■ Uses speech or noncrying sounds to get and keep attention ■ Uses gestures to communicate (waving, holding arms to be picked up) ■ Imitates different speech sounds ■ Has one or two words (hi, dog, dada, mama) around first birthday, although sounds may not be clear

What Should My Child Be Able to Do? One to Two Years	
Hearing and Understanding	**Talking**
■ Points to a few body parts when asked. ■ Follows simple commands and understands simple questions ("Roll the ball," "Kiss the baby," "Where's your shoe?"). ■ Listens to simple stories, songs, and rhymes. ■ Points to pictures in a book when named.	■ Says more words every month. ■ Uses some one- or two-word questions ("Where kitty?" "Go bye-bye?" "What's that?"). ■ Puts two words together ("more cookie," "no juice," "mommy book"). ■ Uses many different consonant sounds at the beginning of words.

What Should My Child Be Able to Do? Two to Three Years	
Hearing and Understanding	**Talking**
■ Understands differences in meaning ("go-stop," "in-on," "big-little," "up-down"). ■ Follows two requests ("Get the book and put it on the table"). ■ Listens to and enjoys hearing stories for longer periods of time.	■ Has a word for almost everything. ■ Uses two or three words to talk about and ask for things. ■ Uses *k, g, f, t, d,* and *n* sounds. ■ Speech is understood by familiar listeners most of the time. ■ Often asks for or directs attention to objects by naming them.

What Should My Child Be Able to Do? Three to Four Years	
Hearing and Understanding	**Talking**
■ Hears you when you call from another room. ■ Hears television or radio at the same loudness level as other family members. ■ Answers simple "who?", "what?", "where?", and "why?" questions.	■ Talks about activities at school or at friends' homes. ■ People outside of the family usually understand child's speech. ■ Uses a lot of sentences that have 4 or more words. ■ Usually talks easily without repeating syllables or words.

What Should My Child Be Able to Do? Four to Five Years	
Hearing and Understanding	**Talking**
■ Pays attention to a short story and answers simple questions about it. ■ Hears and understands most of what is said at home and in school.	■ Uses sentences that give lots of details ("The biggest peach is mine"). ■ Tells stories that stick to topic. ■ Communicates easily with other children and adults. ■ Says most sounds correctly except a few like *l, s, r, v, z, ch, sh, th*. ■ Says rhyming words. ■ Names some letters and numbers. ■ Uses the same grammar as the rest of the family.

This table reprinted with permission from the website of the American Speech-Language-Hearing Association: www.asha.org.

References

American Speech-Language-Hearing Association. How does your child hear and talk? www.ASHA.org/public/speech/development/chart.htm.

Carr, E.G. & Durand, V.M. (1985). Reducing behavior problems through functional communication training. *Journal of Applied Behavior Analysis 18,* 111-26.

Delmolino, L. & Harris, S. (2004). *Incentives for Change: Motivating People with Autism Spectrum Disorders to Learn and Gain Independence.* Bethesda, MD: Woodbine House.

Glasberg, B. (2005). *Functional Behavior Assessment for People with Autism: Making Sense of Seemingly Senseless Behavior.* Bethesda, MD: Woodbine House.

Hart, B. & Risley, T.R. (2002). *Meaningful Differences in the Everyday Experience of Young American Children.* Baltimore: Paul H. Brookes Publishing Company.

Kasari, C., Freeman, S. & Paparella, T. (2006). Joint attention and symbolic play in young children with autism: A randomized controlled intervention study. *Journal of Child Psychology and Psychiatry 47,* 611-20.

Murray, D.S., Creaghead, N.A., Manning-Courtney, P., Shear, P.K., Bean, J. & Prendeville, J. (2008). The relationship between joint attention and language in children with autism spectrum disorders. *Focus on Autism and Other Developmental Disabilities. 23*, 1, 5-14.

Partington, J. W. (2006). *The Assessment of Basic Language and Learning Skills-Revised (ABLLS-R).* Pleasant Hill, CA: Behavior Analysts, Inc.

Partington, J. & Sundberg, M.L. (1998). *The Assessment of Basic Language and Learning Skills (ABLLS).* Pleasant Hill, CA: Behavior Analysts, Inc.

Sundberg, M.L. (2008).*Verbal Behavior Milestones Assessment and Placement Program (VB-MAPP).* Concord, CA: AVB Press.

Taylor, B. A. & Hoch, H. (2008). Teaching children with autism to respond to and to initiate bids for joint attention. *Journal of Applied Behavior Analysis 41,* 377-91.

5 Introduction to Social Language

Owen

Owen is a three-and-a-half-year-old boy with autism. He has made excellent progress in all areas of his curriculum. He mands frequently and in many different situations. For example, he requests information when he needs or desires more specific instructions or details, and he asks to get out of activities that are unpleasant or boring. His mands are often spontaneous, even in these broader contexts.

However, aside from manding, Owen is not particularly strong at initiating communication. For all other kinds of interactions, Owen generally simply waits for others to ask him a question or give him a direction. Owen's team is concerned that he is overly passive. They have noticed that he does not initiate any conversations and does not even comment to others when he is with them.

They have decided to work on tacting, in the hope that Owen will begin commenting in natural situations. They hope that teaching tacting will serve as a bridge to spontaneous commenting and to initiating social exchanges.

Doug

Doug is a four-year-old boy with Asperger's disorder who has made excellent progress in all areas. He is above age level in all academic areas. He has never had any difficulty with communication skills, and his issues with speech are extremely subtle. (He has some difficulties understanding figurative language such as idioms and expressions. For example, he does not understand exaggerations or common expressions such as "I'm so hungry I could eat a horse.")

Doug's major challenge stems not from the mechanics of communication (the "how") but from the content of communication (the "what"). Doug is extremely interested in trains. While this may seem like an excellent area of interest for a four-year-old boy, Doug's interests are idiosyncratic and unusual. Instead of being interested in Thomas the Tank Engine, Doug is interested in light rail transportation technology, in how coal is used to power steam locomotive engines, and in exactly how many miles per hour different types of trains travel.

Sometimes Doug can engage other children in conversation about trains that is of some interest to them. (He will discuss Thomas and all of Thomas's train friends, for example.) However, Doug always wants to take the conversation to areas of content that are of no interest to his listeners. Doug does not pick up on the social cues that his listeners send about their lack of interest.

Furthermore, Doug's team has become concerned about the increasing intensity of his preoccupation with these topics. It has become more difficult to redirect Doug from talking about trains. In fact, he now sometimes actively resists redirection, and may become agitated and flustered. He is also trying to steer conversations in the directions of his special interests more and more. Doug's peers seem irritated by this pattern and are starting to avoid Doug.

Doug's team wants to ensure that his interest in trains doesn't become so intense that it interferes with his ability to talk about other things. They want to make sure that the power of his interest does not discourage his peers from approaching him and interacting with him. They are hoping to increase Doug's flexibility in conversation and improve his ability to control his talk about trains.

Abigail

Abigail is a three-year-old girl who was diagnosed with autism right before her second birthday. She has made excellent progress in an ABA program. When intervention started, she spent much of her time screaming and engaged in tantrums. She had no way to get her needs met and could not communicate effectively. When she was frustrated, she often bit her cuticles and picked her skin.

Abigail's ABA team focused initially on two major goals. The first goal was to simply increase Abigail's approaches to her instructors. In the beginning, Abigail would usually run screaming from them, and would resist any attempt they made to interact. Consequently, the team members set out to make sure Abigail viewed them as a source of fun and shared enjoyment. They worked hard to pair themselves with preferred activities and items, allowing her to have access to them at any time, and constantly expanded the range of activities and items they offered her.

The team's second goal was to build Abigail's ability to request items and activities. Initially, they taught her to mand using the Picture Exchange Communication System (PECS). When she exchanged a card, she received an item or activity she desired. Whenever Abigail gave them a card, they also modeled the vocal language for her. For example, when Abigail handed them a card with the sentence strip "I want a cookie," the instructor would say, "I want a cookie" as she gave Abigail the cookie. Abigail soon began vocalizing along with her card exchanges, and eventually her vocal requests supplanted the use of PECS.

Abigail's manding was strong in some ways. She requested a wide range of items and activities and even requested preferred items when they were not in her view. However, she did not request anything other than preferred items and activities. For example, she did not request attention and she did not ask for help with difficult tasks.

Abigail's team felt strongly that her manding repertoire could be strengthened, and that this would greatly increase her independence.

Ethan

Ethan is a three-and-a-half-year-old boy with autism. While Ethan has developed many skills, he has not become a vocal communicator. He is quite adept at using the Picture Exchange Communication System, and he readily requests things he wants and needs via PECS. He can discriminate between pictures well, he can search through multiple pages of his book to find the picture he wants, and he can travel to find the person he wants to interact with. He requests social interactions and games as well as tangible items.

Ethan shows a lot of social interest, and he wants to communicate with his peers. However, his peers do not know how to respond to his PECS communications. Ethan's book is always available to him, and he has full and complete access to it at all times. Even so, there are times when Ethan can't immediately or easily access his book and times when communication is a challenge. Examples include when he is involved in sensory activities (e.g., water table), when the class is swimming, and when he is involved in an outdoor game.

Ethan's team members want to ensure that Ethan can be fully social and engaged with his peers, and that his communication modality will not limit or inhibit his interactions. They want to think creatively about how he can communicate in these more difficult situations. They also want to come up with ideas to help his peers understand his communications.

Joshua

Joshua, a three-and-a-half-year-old boy with autism, has strong receptive and expressive language skills, and he communicates well and spontaneously. Joshua's problem is that he is a slow responder, a child who requires "processing time." He has been described as having auditory processing deficits. The teachers working with Joshua have always considered Joshua's slow response times to be just part of who Joshua is.

However, they now notice all the ways in which this slow style limits him. It is not unusual for Joshua to take 7 to 10 seconds to reply to a peer's greeting, question, or invitation to play. Similarly, it can take him up to 10 seconds to answer the teacher in a group. Often, he misses the chance to socially connect or to participate in the group because the lag time has been too long.

Teachers have also noticed that Joshua is often a step behind his friends in following instructions. If a teacher gives instructions for a multistep task, he is often at least one step behind the rest of the class. He never finishes his craft projects or the simple worksheets handed out in class.

Joshua's team realizes that this slowness will affect his independence in a classroom environment. They also realize that the gap will widen between him and other students as his peers become even more adept at processing information and instructions. They would like to explore how they can help Joshua to respond faster in all situations requiring receptive language and expressive communication.

Horatio

Horatio is a four-year-old boy with Asperger's disorder who is very "high-functioning." He is well above other children his age in nearly every area. He can read, do simple addition, and write words. He can follow instructions in a group situation, can attend to teacher directions, and can follow along with the group.

Horatio's challenges occur in situations that involve social rules. While he can play simple games such as tag quite well, he struggles when games become more complex. He also becomes upset if a game is played with slightly different rules that he is used to. He gets extremely upset at these times, and may accuse his friends of playing "wrong" or of "cheating."

When upset, Horatio often reacts quite strongly and immediately. He may become argumentative or aggressive, and it is quite difficult to calm him down. His teachers have tried to help Horatio understand that there are many different options for dealing with being upset, but he often simply reacts without thinking.

Because of these behaviors, other children are losing interest in playing with Horatio. They see him as unpredictable and as a "sore loser." Horatio also often fails to respond appropriately to peers when they are upset or hurt. He can appear oblivious or even uncaring. All of these characteristics taken together have made social integration a little tougher than other goals.

Horatio's team members want to address all of the issues that are interacting here—social, language, and behavioral challenges. They are aware that Horatio has an excellent chance of being well-served in inclusive education. However, they also see how his difficulties could seriously limit the success of this experience. They want to help Horatio to find the right words at the right time and to control his behavior.

What These Scenarios Tell Us

All of these scenarios describe challenges that can arise for children with autism spectrum disorders in the social use of language. Communication happens in a social context. The social and communication challenges faced by children with autism interact, and the deficits in communicating make it harder to build and maintain friendships and relationships. The ways in which social language deficits present themselves are probably as numerous as individuals with autism themselves! The cases above, however, illustrate many of the commonly encountered pitfalls:

- Owen can mand readily, but doesn't spontaneously interact in any other way. Unless he is requesting something, he does not initiate a social interaction.

- Doug can speak readily and easily, but the content of his speech is ritualistic. He is overly interested in details and mechanics of trains, in a way that others find off-putting, odd, and uninteresting. He has difficulty demonstrating the flexibility essential to the back-and-forth flow of conversation. He also is becoming more rigid about controlling conversational topics, and his intolerance is leading to more challenging behaviors.
- Abigail can request needed items, but she doesn't ask to get other kinds of desires met. She remains dependent on others to anticipate her needs and desires. She needs to be more independent in spontaneously requesting many things in order to succeed in a setting with reduced teacher attention.
- Ethan has difficulties with social communication because of modality issues. Although he uses PECS very competently, he can't use it everywhere he needs to communicate.
- Joshua has trouble keeping up with the pace of social conversation and interactions. Although he can express himself well through speech, he responds very slowly when others speak to him.
- Horatio has extremely good expressive language skills, but he exhibits subtle deficits in social understanding that make it difficult for him to communicate effectively, to react empathically, and to play flexibly.

Each scenario points out the significant interplay among language skills, social understanding, and behavioral control. Often, these factors influence each other and create significant challenges for youngsters with ASD who are learning to communicate.

Language Is Social

It is hard to discuss language separate from socialization. In many ways, the distinction between the two areas is artificial or arbitrary. In fact, when we examine the evolution of language in typically developing youngsters, we see that it is largely socially focused. Think back to the basic functions of language discussed in earlier chapters:

- Sometimes children communicate to request (mand). Often, they are manding for specific items and activities, but they may also mand for help, attention, and escape from difficult demands.
- Children also communicate to convey something they are experiencing in their environment (i.e., something they smell, hear, see, or taste). These comments are called tacts. While they involve making contact with the environment (as Skinner noted), they also involve making contact with another person about one's experience. Tacting essentially involves shared experience. Children comment on the sight of a clown or the sound of rain and expect their conversational partner to react to their observations.
- Children also speak just to converse, simply enjoying the back-and-forth conversational exchange that characterizes reciprocal conversation.

All of these examples meet the definition of verbal behavior. Reinforcement is provided via the response of another person. Much of the reinforcement derived from communication exchanges is social; it involves connection, attention, and reciprocal sharing.

There is a tremendous amount of social motivation involved in communication. Most of what we shared with others is done for social reasons. Individuals with autism are far less socially motivated than typically developing individuals. For them, manding is generally the easiest function of communication, as well as the easiest communication skill to strengthen, because requests are associated with the receipt of preferred activities and items. That is, the child with autism gets something concrete out of making requests, not just social reinforcement.

Still, the more socially complex forms of manding are sometimes difficult to teach. This may be due, in part, to the social aspects of the requests. For example, asking for information involves figuring out whom to ask and what kind of information to request, while asking for help requires finding an appropriate person to ask for help.

Tacting is very difficult for most individuals with autism to achieve because it is basically motivated by the desire to share experience. Spontaneous tacting is particularly uncommon among children with autism spectrum disorders.

The verbal behavior that B.F. Skinner named the intraverbal presents numerous challenges for children with autism. As discussed in Chapter 2, intraverbals involve conversation or back-and-forth exchanges. Much of what happens in conversation involves tuning into the cues of others. However, nonverbal communications are largely not perceived by individuals with autism. As a result, they may miss information about their conversational partner's interest level or availability to converse. In addition, children with autism do best when answering questions and responding to specific instructions or inquiries. However, much of what occurs in the context of conversations requires reacting to information given as statements, offering similar information, asking follow-up questions, and otherwise adding to the conversational thread. These conversational skills are far weaker in the vast majority of people with autism.

In the next chapter, we will discuss some of the ways in which social language in young children can be fostered to both improve communication and foster social connections. We will also review some of the ways to collect data and evaluate progress in these areas.

6 Strategies for Developing and Promoting the Use of Social Language

Language and Social Skills

As we explained in the previous chapter, the distinction between social skills and language skills is artificial in many ways. Communication is a social process. To be socially competent, one must be able to effectively communicate.

Some of the communication skills we have discussed so far are necessary social survival skills. For example, being able to request needed or wanted items is essential for independent functioning. Other skills we have discussed are thoroughly social in nature, such as making simple conversational overtures.

As we have reviewed, typically developing children learn to communicate their basic wants and needs and to use their language abilities to create social connections. They also learn communication skills that make them more successful in social contexts. That is, they figure out the words that work well in social situations, making them effective communicators and preferred play partners. They learn to ask for turns in games, to request that a friend share materials, and to make relevant comment when acting out pretend play scenarios with other children. These language skills are social skills; they help children to be more successful in playing with their friends and following with the group.

For children with autism, it is often difficult to develop these skills. They fail to perceive the social cues that help orient and guide other children. They also have difficulty understanding social information offered by others. The demands of social situations are significant for children with autism. Often, they avoid social situations because it is so difficult for them to understand the social requirements and expectations.

Joint Attention

Some children are initially referred for an evaluation of autism spectrum disorder when they fail to acquire communication skills at the expected rate. Many children, however, are referred because of some subtle differences in how they are making social connections. A common problem observed in children with autism at this early age is a lack of ***joint attention.***

Joint attention skills typically develop before a child's first words. In recent years, joint attention has received a great deal of attention because it may have important implications for both early diagnosis and intervention (Bruinsma, Koegel, & Koegel, 2004). The term joint attention can be difficult to define because it encompasses a variety of skills (e.g., gaze following, social referencing). Descriptions of joint attention often include terms such as "sharing attention" or "knowing what another person is looking at and experiencing." The simplest everyday example involves a toddler pointing at objects she wants her parent to notice. (Think about the child pointing to an airplane when on a walk with his or her mother.)

For this book, joint attention will be defined as a coordinated shift in attention between an object or event and another person, which occurs in a social context. The term is used to refer to both recruiting (or initiating) attention and responding to others' bids for attention. For instance, a child recruiting attention may point to a toy while saying, "Look," or may reach for a toy while turning to an adult for help. Other examples include a child responding to bids for attention from others, turning to look when she hears her name called, or looking back and forth from a toy being held out to the person holding it. Children with autism typically have significant deficits in joint attention, with difficulties both in initiating requests for joint attention and responding to others' bids for joint attention.

There are two main types of bids for attention: 1) protoimperative, and 2) protodeclarative (Whalen and Shreibman, 2003). While both types may look similar, they serve different purposes.

We use ***protoimperative*** gestures and vocalizations to request access to an object. For example, a child may point to the refrigerator when she wants juice or pick up her shoes to show she wants to go outside. When a child makes these kinds of requests, she is essentially manding, and is looking to the other person to meet her need by providing the desired item.

We use ***protodeclarative*** gestures and vocalizations to attract another person's attention for sharing an experience or to ensure mutual attending to an object. For example, a child may point to a duck on a pond or to a silly clown. She does not want the duck or clown, but simply wants her parent to see the same thing. This type of initiation is a request to share experience.

All of these very technical definitions really point to two basic distinctions. First, there is a significant difference between initiating joint attention and responding to others' requests to attend. In one case, the person is simply responding to another person's request to notice something and to share an experience. In the other case, she is asking someone to notice something and to join them in attending to it. Second, there is a qualitative difference between requests for desired items and requests to share experience. Shared experience is more socially complex than a manding interaction. Children with autism usually have much more difficulty with gaining someone's attention to share an experience than they do with requesting desired items.

Importance of Joint Attention

Researchers have found that learning joint attention skills helps children develop skills in a number of other areas. These include:

- language development,
- adaptive social-emotional behavioral development such as play skills (Sheinkopf, Mundy, Claussen, & Willoughby, 2004),
- frontal lobe function (Mundy & Crowson, 1997), important for problem-solving, and
- vocabulary development. For instance, one group of researchers found that time spent engaging in joint attention behaviors was positively related to the child's later vocabulary size (Bruinsma, Koegel, and Koegel , 2004) and another group found that response to joint attention was directly related to vocabulary development in children between six and twenty-four months of age (Morales, Mundy, Delgado, Yale, Messinger, Neal, and Schwartz, 2000).

Given the language and communication deficits that are characteristic of children with autism, joint attention is an especially important skill for them to acquire. Any skill that can increase vocabulary is very valuable, as vocabulary is the foundation on which complex listening skills, spontaneous tacting (labeling), and conversation are built. Likewise, boosting your child's ability to share experiences with others can have tremendous social significance. Consequently, the next sections will summarize strategies that can be used to teach these skills to children with autism.

Research on Teaching Joint Attention

There is some evidence that joint attention skills may be teachable. In one recent study, children with autism were assigned to one of three experimental groups: a group that was specifically taught joint attention skills, a group that was taught symbolic play skills, and a control group (Kasari, Freeman, and Paparella, 2006). The researchers provided treatment consisting largely of discrete trial training, shaping, and naturalistic teaching procedures. After five to six weeks of daily sessions, both treatment groups made improvements in joint attention and joint engagement. Perhaps most importantly, the children also generalized their improved skills to interactions with their caregivers.

In a similar study, the authors compared the effects of different interventions (joint attention intervention, symbolic play intervention) on expressive language in three- and four-year-olds with autism (Kasari, Paparella, Freeman, and Jahromi, 2008). They found gains in expressive language for both the joint attention and symbolic play intervention groups. These gains increased over time, as shown in a twelve-month follow-up. This suggests that there are significant and lasting benefits of including joint attention training and symbolic play training when teaching young children with autism.

Joint attention interventions are compelling because of their social and communicative significance. If we can target the core deficit in joint attention with our teaching, the magnitude of socially significant change may be much greater. However, the real test of these teaching procedures will be in how well the skills transfer to the natural environment and how well children maintain them over time. It is expected that we will learn more about how to foster and generalize these skills over the next several years.

Some Novel Ways to Increase Joint Attention

In teaching joint attention to children with autism, we must remember that we notice things that are interesting to us. We do not point out paper clips or rubber bands to our coworkers. Children do not point out spoons or blankets. We try to get others to pay attention to things that are interesting, novel, pretty, fun, or preferred.

Recently, researcher Bridget Taylor has capitalized on this natural tendency to want to share interesting and novel experiences by setting up the environment so that children feel compelled to either respond to or initiate joint attention (Taylor, 2009). For example, a large Sponge Bob character may drop from the ceiling. The child is taught to notice the interesting event, and to point it out to someone else.

It is important that such interventions use truly unusual events and highly interesting items to entice the child into sharing social exchanges with others. In selecting items for teaching this skill to individual children, consider their preferences and interests. Table 6.1 lists some objects and activities that children with autism might find interesting enough to want to share with others.

Table 6-1 | Activities and Items That Might Be Used to Teach Joint Attention

- Items encountered on outdoor walks
  - Flowers
  - Animals
  - The moon at night
  - Airplane and jet lines (contrails)
  - Clouds
  - Insects
  - Puddles
  - Rain
  - Snow
- Places encountered on community outings
  - Pet stores
  - Firehouses
  - Libraries
  - Police stations
- Favorite characters (movie, TV, book, cartoon)
- Pictures of favorite places
  - Parks
  - Disney
  - The beach
  - Vacation spots
  - Carnivals
  - Pools and water parks
- Favorite foods
  - Visiting restaurants to sample
  - Pictures of favorite restaurants
  - Pictures of favorite foods
- Special interest items (examples of preferred items—always tailored to individual child's preferences)
  - Thomas the Tank Trains
  - Solar system pictures
  - Disney characters
  - Maps
  - Rocks

How Can Parents Help?

To use novel and interesting activities or items to teach your child joint attention skills, you can take advantage of opportunities in your daily routine as they arise or plan out an activity in which you hope to work on joint attention skills.

To use opportunities as they arise, you need to be aware of what kinds of things truly interest your child. In other words, do not try to get her to look at something that she doesn't care about (i.e., don't cry wolf too often or your child will learn that it's not worth looking when you say "look!"). For example, let's say that you know your child likes cats and you come across a cat sunning itself on the sidewalk. If your child is clearly interested in the cat and you want her to make a bid for your attention, you could prompt her to point out the cat to you. You can do this explicitly by gesturing to the cat or by physically helping your child to point to the cat. Then you react with pleasure. You could also script it for your child, providing a joint communication statement such as "Wow, look at that!"

Another strategy is to simply stop and look very expectantly at your child, waiting for her to notice the cat. In responding to your child's bids for attention, be sure to include both vocal and nonvocal responses. We do not always solicit or respond to joint attention with vocal responses; we often merely sigh, smile, or look expectantly. To help your children generalize those skills well into natural interactions, think broadly about different kinds of reactions to model for her.

Alternately, *you* could initiate the bid for your child's attention and work on her response to your bid. To achieve shared attention, you might first want to establish eye contact with your child and then point to and look at the cat from a close distance (perhaps three to five feet away). Then look back at your child to ensure she sees the cat. If she does not follow your gaze, get as close to the cat as possible, and repeat the procedure.)

Sometimes you might want to set up situations in which you can work on joint attention skills with your child. For example, you might plan a trip specifically to a place that you know will be very interesting to your child (e.g., a train station). Or you might purchase or borrow an item from a library or friend that is related to one of her special interests.

There is some research suggesting that using your child's perseverative interests may be a good starting place when trying to increase her motivation to initiate joint attention (Vismara & Lyons, 2007). That is, if you can set up a situation involving one of your child's interests, your child may see that interest as a motivational reward for entering into a social interaction with you. This is in keeping with the reason that typically developing children initiate joint attention—to share an experience rather than to obtain something.

The main precaution in working with your child on joint attention is to remember what joint attention is all about. It is about *interest.* We share interesting things and experiences, and we seek to share items and activities that are novel, fun, and high interest. If your child shows displeasure or disinterest when you are trying to get her to initiate or respond to bids for attention, it is not a good context for teaching these skills.

Greetings

People expect even very young children to be able to wave "hi" and "bye. The inability to do this, or a lack of responsiveness to greetings, can be very socially stigmatizing. Conversely, if a child can make and respond to greetings, it will often lead to more interactions in the context of play. For these reasons, greetings are an important part of early instruction for children with autism.

Within ABA programs, children are often explicitly taught to use greetings with discrete trial programs as well as in natural contexts. For example, your child might be taught to answer a person who is saying "Hi" by making eye contact and waving. To help children generalize the skill, we look for ways to practice greetings in the real world. For example, in school, opportunities for using and responding to greetings occur many times per day, as students enter the class, return from activities, meet visitors, or go on errands to other parts of the school. At home, parents can capitalize on many naturally occurring opportunities for greetings, such as visits from friends and extended family, the delivery of mail, trips to the bus stop, the return of parents from work, etc.

In the beginning stages of teaching greetings, you want to focus mostly on getting your child to respond to others' greetings with a wave. Later, you can focus on teaching your child to initiate greetings with a wave. Even later still, you can begin to attend to nuances of greetings, such as pairing a wave with eye contact, including some kind of vocal greeting with a wave, or responding to others' greetings more quickly. This last issue is related to fluency, a concept discussed in Chapter 9.

Early Conversation Skills

Conversation skills are the most socially oriented language skills of all. When we engage in conversation, we are not usually trying to obtain access to a specific object or activity, as we are when we make requests (mand), and we are not just labeling things in our environment, as we do when we tact.

As explained in Chapter 2, conversation skills or intraverbals can best be understood as the aspect of language that addresses to-and-fro exchanges. That is, intraverbals deal with answering questions, conversing, and, in particular, talking about things or events that are not present, such as what you did over the weekend, where you went on vacation, or what movie you saw. For example, if someone says, "Where the Wild Things Are" in response to the question, "What movie did you see this week-

end?" it would be considered an intraverbal response. You can only imagine all the different types of questions and answers that could be generated with an intraverbal repertoire.

Making conversation is extremely difficult for most young children with autism. This is not only because they often have trouble learning to use expressive language to communicate their wants, needs, and thoughts. It is also because they have problems with social comprehension—with understanding the reasons that people communicate socially. Many potential social opportunities are lost because children with autism do not even perceive certain events as social opportunities. For example, they often do not spontaneously comment on things or respond to comments offered that are not framed as questions. In short, they frequently do not know whether, what, or how to say things to others.

The next section discusses the first method that is often used in ABA programs to help young children with autism spectrum disorders learn to participate in back-and-forth exchanges with others—the fill-in.

Fill-ins

When working with very young children with autism spectrum disorders, it is important to understand when intraverbals can be taught, as well as in what progression to introduce them. One of the first types of intraverbals we teach is the fill-in. Fill-ins are considered a version of intraverbal responding, but have more to do with *completing* or *filling-in* a word or phrase to a statement than independently coming up with a conversational response.

Parents often use fill-ins with young children when they sing a well-known song , recite a nursery rhyme, or read a favorite book and wait for the child to finish the sentence. For example, a parent might sing, "The Wheels on the . . ." and hold out for her child to say "bus." As soon as the child fills in the sentence, the parent usually provides social and educational reinforcement (such as by smiling and saying "that's right") and the singing continues on. Another example of a fill-in is saying, "A doggie says . . . " and waiting for the child to say "woof woof."

Typically, fill-ins are less difficult to teach and are more developmentally appropriate for children who have very limited or no intraverbal repertoires. Remember that even typically developing children spend a lot of time initially filling in words to songs, fun activities, and animal sounds before moving on to answering true questions such as "What's your name?" and "How old are you?"

Using the Fill-in Procedure with Your Child

How do you choose the fill-ins to teach? There are a couple of major, important variables. The most important consideration is your child's interest. What songs does she prefer? What stories does she know by heart? What books does she know lines from? What nursery rhymes do you frequently recite? It is important to use high interest and strongly preferred material. Another important consideration is articulation ability. How well can your child say the fill-in words or an acceptable approximation? In general, we want to program for success, so do not choose a word that is impossible for your child to say.

The teaching procedure is simple. Children are used to the lines of songs and nursery rhymes, and will often fill in naturally. You can use a time delay strategy, in which you wait for your child to finish the line or sentence. If a few seconds elapse without your child filling in the missing word, provide a model for her. If your child does fill in the word, strongly reinforce her. Even if the topic is something your child prefers, she is learning a new skill, involving retrieving and saying the right word. Therefore, you should lavishly reward that effort.

If you are collecting data on the procedure (see "Data Collection" on page 122, you can track the percentage of time your child independently fills in the word (vs. requiring help).

The fill-in format can be used with many activities. In addition to nursery rhymes and songs, you can use it for:

- common activities (e.g., "to go outside we need our socks and ____.")
- animal sounds (e.g., "A cow says ____") and
- functions of objects ("A cup is for____") .

Note that when using fill-ins, the child is not just retrieving a word from a song or poem that she has heard many times. Instead, she must search her vocabulary for the right word and then produce it. In the beginning, your child may need lots of prompts to say the word. Later, you can fade back the prompt and just give the first sound of the expected response. Likewise, if your child is using PECS or sign to communicate, she may initially need physical or gestural prompts to perform or select the correct response.

Answering Who, What, Where Questions

Once a child has a relatively strong fill-in repertoire, questions involving *What, Who, and Where* can be introduced. Often, these questions begin simply as requests to label items (e.g., "What is this?"). It can then extend into functions of items (e.g., "What is a cup for?"), categories (e.g., "What is a bird?"), and more complex Wh- questions (e.g., "Where do you buy groceries?").

As with most skills taught in ABA programs, prompting will be used to help your child learn how to answer Wh- questions. For example, here is how a child who can imitate words might be prompted to answer a question about function:

1. Instructor says to child, "Say ball."
2. Child says "ball."
3. Instructor says, "What do you bounce?" (and prompts child to say "ball").
4. Child says "ball."
5. Instructor follows up with a phonemic prompt, asking, "What do you bounce? Say B …."
6. Child says "ball."
7. Instructor follows up once more with only the question, "What do you bounce?"
8. Child says "ball."

More Complex Intraverbals

Later, intraverbals become more complex as children learn to comment on the content of others' words. For example, one child might say, "I have Pringles for snack" and another might reply, "I have Cheetos for snack today." In later childhood, typically developing children learn to have an entire discussion in which they describe an event such as a birthday party or a trip to the zoo with mom and dad.

We use many teaching strategies to help children on the autism spectrum develop these conversational skills. Of course, we rely on modeling and prompting. Often, we target highly preferred items for conversational exchanges.

Conversation requires commenting and responding to comments, so this becomes a major focus of instruction. In other words, children must not simply learn to answer questions, but must also learn to reply

to comments and offer comments of their own. The easiest way to do this is with simple reciprocal information exchanges (e.g., Partner 1: "My name is Lindsey." Partner 2: "My name is Julia.") The length of these conversational exchanges can be increased over time, and varied across topics. This is often done by setting goals for a specific number of back-and-forth conversational exchanges (e.g., 1 exchange, 2 exchanges, 3 exchanges, etc.). In addition, we also rely on strategies such as scripting and video modeling (described below) to increase the length, complexity, and variability of conversation.

Some children may initially be taught to have longer conversations through the use of visual prompts such as pictures arranged in a sequence (for example, showing events at a birthday party or a trip to the zoo). A parent might then ask her child to tell about the birthday party while prompting her child to describe each picture arranged in a picture book. For example, "On Sunday my friend Nora came to my house. We played with balloons. We sang happy birthday and blew out candles. Then we ate some cake. I also opened up presents." Each description or "intraverbal" by the child might be in response to a simple question asked by her parent. ("What did you do on Sunday?" "What did you play with?" "Did you have a cake with candles?" "Did you get some cool presents?").

Children can also be taught to ask various questions in addition to responding to questions. In our example above, a child might be taught to say, "What did you do on Sunday?" after hearing the comment, "I did something exciting this weekend!"

Social Comprehension

Social comprehension is a term that has been used to describe the complicated social responses and initiations that are part of navigating the social world. It includes understanding social rules, behaving as expected in given contexts, and interpreting social nuances. Social comprehension skills are essential for making meaningful progress and are difficult to define and teach.

There are a number of commercially available curricula that target the development of these skills and that have well-formulated lessons (e.g., Baker, 2003a; 2003b; McGuiness & Goldstein, 1990; Richardson, 1996; Taylor & Jasper, 2001). Many of these curricula are written by behavior analysts, and outline methodical teaching strategies and the collection of data to guide decisions. They are extremely useful resources for the identification of, and instruction in, social skills.

Often, a variety of strategies are used together, in a packaged approach, to help children with autism increase their social comprehension. Such packages may combine both strategies proven to be effective in research (empirically validated) and nonempirically validated techniques. Commonly used components of such packages include:

- video modeling,
- Social Stories,
- rule cards, and
- role plays.

Many parents and teachers have learned to use one or more of these techniques with children with autism spectrum disorders. We will review each of these strategies below.

Video Modeling

Many students with ASD are strong visual learners, and often enjoy watching videos. They may attend better to a model presented in a video clip than to a live model demonstrating a skill. Video modeling capitalizes on a child's visual learning skills and her interest in watching videos.

There are two types of video modeling that are used with people with autism and other developmental disabilities:

1. ***video modeling***—in which an adult or peer serves as the model, and
2. ***video self-modeling***—in which the child herself serves as the model.

Video modeling usually involves having the child observe a video clip of the desired actions, such as playing with a toy house, pretending to get a haircut, or building a castle with blocks. Video modeling is often done with an adult demonstrating the skill first. Using an adult model makes it easier to ensure that the salient aspects of the target behavior will be highlighted. Older peer tutors or mature peers can also be used as models. The advantage of using peers is that they are closer in age to the child. They may even be the same children that the child will be interacting with.

Prompting procedures are used to help the child engage in the skill or behavior demonstrated in the video. Initially, the child may be prompted to simultaneously imitate what she is watching (doing the actions along with the model on tape). Next, the child may be prompted to imitate what she observed after the video is over (watching the clip and then engaging in the play). When working on communication skills, a conversational partner may be present while the child watches the video. This enables the child to immediately imitate the communication skills demonstrated on the video, although delayed imitation is the ultimate goal.

Rote responding can be a significant concern when using video instruction. Children with autism may learn just one way of playing, conversing, etc. They can insist on following a script, on doing the action exactly and only as it has been shown to them. This makes it essential to program variability into the video modeling protocol. In other words, the team may make several different videos of the same activity with slight differences in content and in the sequences of actions. This can help ensure that the child learns to imitate and not simply to memorize the clip.

Video Self-Review: An extension of video instruction is to use videotape as a source of feedback to children on their performance during play activities. This technique is often called video self-review. Using this procedure, the child watches a video of herself in action, much as a football player might watch a video of himself at practice in an attempt to improve his performance. While the child is watching the video, reinforcement and corrective feedback can be provided. The teacher might guide the child's observation with pointed questions: "Were you looking at your friend?" "Did your answer make sense?"

An adult or peer can then model better strategies for targeted areas of weakness and rehearse them with the child (e.g., Taylor,

2001). This strategy might have special relevance for children who have demonstrated difficulty comprehending social nuances, such as staying on topic in a conversation.

Video Self-Modeling: Video self-modeling is a variation of video modeling in which the child watches a film of herself performing the desired behavior or skill. If the child seldom engages in the behavior, she may need to be filmed for an extended period of time in order to capture the rare instances when she performs the skill. The video is then edited down so that only the target skill is shown to the child. Or if the child only performs the behavior with prompts, she may be prompted to do the skill, and then the prompts are edited out of the video.

Sometimes a video may even be made of the child performing at a slightly higher level than she usually does in order to help her see that she is capable of a more advanced skill. For example, if a child customarily speaks in one-word utterances, a number of her spoken words may be recorded and then cut and pasted together with video editing software so that she is shown speaking several two-word phrases.

Researchers including Peter Dowrick, who pioneered the method, and Tom Buggey have found that teachers, parents, and others can learn to make self-modeling videos that help children with autism or other disabilities learn a range of behaviors, from answering questions, to increasing reading skills, to interacting more appropriately with peers. For more information on the method, you may wish to read *Seeing Is Believing: Video Self-Modeling for People with Autism and Other Developmental Disabilities* (Buggey, 2009).

Research on Video Modeling

Several studies have shown that video modeling can be an effective tool for teaching people with autism. Video modeling has been shown to be useful for teaching the imitation of peers (Haring, Kennedy, Adams, & Pitts-Conway, 1987), learning sign language (Watkins, Sprafkin, & Krolikowski, 1993), developing play skills (Charlop-Christy, Le, & Freeman, 2000), and building conversation skills (Charlop & Milstein, 1989; Sherer et al., 2001). Because so much research supports its usefulness in teaching skills, video modeling is increasingly being used to build a variety of skills, including functional academic skills, community-relevant skills, conversational exchanges, and play skills (e. g., Snell & Brown, 2000; Taylor, 2001; Weiss & Harris, 2001).

Several guidelines for using video with children with autism have been given (e. g., Krantz, MacDuff, Wadstrom, & McClannahan, 1991). Suggestions include:

- First, assess the child to see if she has appropriate prerequisite skills. These include having the attention skills to attend to the video and being able to recognize themselves on the video (in the case of video self-modeling).
- Remove extraneous stimuli (background noise, visual distractions) before making the video.
- Take the child's preferences into account when selecting people to present the video or to model skills on video (i.e., use models the child likes or who have positive relationships with her).

Social Stories

As mentioned above, children on the autism spectrum often have difficulty understanding and following the expectations in social situations. Social Stories have become a popular method of conveying some of this social information to people with autism (Barry & Burlew, 2004; Sansosti & Gray, 1998; Powell-Smith & Kincaid, 2004). Social Stories are created for a particular individual to describe a specific situation, challenge, or expectation and involve brief descriptions of expectations that are explained in the context of a "story." Typically, the story is written from the perspective of the person with autism (Gray, 2000) and is read to or with the person before she encounters the situation described in the story. Social stories often include pictures and photos in addition to words (Reynhout & Carter, 2006).

Carol Gray (2000), who is credited with coming up with the idea of Social Stories, has many suggestions for developing Social Stories. Specifically, she has emphasized the importance of using different kinds of sentences that serve different functions. For example, she highlights the importance of sentences that:

- describe the situation to the learner (descriptive),
- provide information about how other people may feel in the situation (perspective),
- state what the learner is expected to do (directive), and
- outline likely consequences associated with different courses of action (consequence). (Barry & Burlew, 2004; Crozier &Tincani, 2007; Reynhout & Carter, 2006).

Social stories can be used both to increase desirable and decrease undesirable behavior. They are often used to:

- help the person acquire skills in situations that may look different each time they are encountered—e.g., lining up for recess, cleaning up after play time, etc.
- help the person deal with situations that provoke fear (dogs, loud noises, or getting a haircut, or going to the dentist)
- reduce challenging behaviors—for instance, by explaining consequences: you can go to the ice cream parlor if you behave at the restaurant; or to explain behavioral alternatives: you can ask for help instead of screaming

For children who need language skills that are needed in social situations, Social Stories might be used to teach how to ask a friend to join a game, how to take turns when playing a simple game, or how to wait your turn to use the slide. See an example of this application in the Sharing Social Story example below.

Researchers have described a variety of approaches for teaching using a Social Story. They include:

- having the teacher or parent read the Social Story to the child (Crozier & Tincani, 2007),

Social Story example

Sharing with My Friends

I have lots of friends at school.

I like to play with my friends.

Sometimes my friends may have a book or toy I want to see.

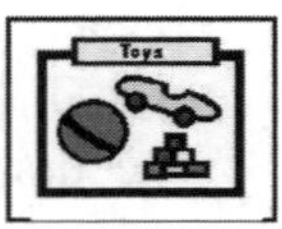

- having the child read (Thiemann & Goldstein, 2001),
- listening or watching the story on a computer or TV (More, 2008; Sansosti & Powell-Smith, 2008), and
- listening to the story in a song (Brownell, 2002).

Implementation is highly variable in nearly every aspect of use.

If you choose to use Social Stories with your child, you may wish to follow the guidelines developed by autism researchers Shannon Crozier and Matthew Tincani (2007). They developed a checklist that provides a clear structure for how to introduce, present, and review Social Stories. Using these guidelines will ensure that everyone involved in reading Social Stories with your child follows a consistent procedure. You will also be able to provide feedback on how well any given individual is using the technique with your child. The critical components of the treatment are:

- having the adult sit across from the child;
- placing the book on the table in front of the child;
- reading the book with the child;
- encouraging the child to look and point at the story;
- telling the child that it's time to do the activity; and
- directing the child to the activity.

[redacted]

Sometimes I take the toy or book and want to keep it .
When this happens it makes my friends feel sad.
If I want to see a toy or book I can say
"Can I see it?"
I need to give the toy or book back to my friends after I am done looking at it.
give
This will make my friends happy.
This will make me happy.

Social Stories can be easily integrated into a preschooler's program of instruction, and are similar to the strategies used with other young children. In general, it is recommended that Social Stories be used in combination with direct behavior change procedures such as prompting and reinforcing the desired behaviors if they are included as part of a package of interventions to teach social language or address other issues.

Research on Social Stories

Although Social Stories are often used with children on the autism spectrum, there have been relatively few carefully controlled investigations into the effectiveness of this method. Most clinical guidelines for using Social Stories have not been empirically validated and require more comprehensive investigation.

Another problem with the research into Social Stories to date is that studies sometimes involve more than one treatment method. For example, one research study used Social Stories in conjunction with text cards (written instructions), visual cues, and video feedback to increase the social and communication skills of five individuals with autism (Thiemann and Goldstein, 2001). The targeted social behaviors included getting attention, making comments, and requesting. Intervention occurred in a small group setting with typical peers along with children with autism. The children's skills improved, but the data on the children's skill maintenance were not impressive.

As previously discussed, Social Stories are often used in combination with other treatments, as part of a packaged social skills intervention (Reynhout & Carter, 2006; Rogers, 2000). When used as part of packaged interventions, some gains have been noted (Sansosti & Powell-Smith, 2008; Swaggart et al., 1995). However, using multiple treatments limits the extent to which effects can be attributed to Social Stories, since it is not clear which components of the treatment packages are responsible for the changes.

Another major challenge in using Social Stories is the lack of information available on the essential elements of their use. There is great variability in how Social Stories are developed, presented to the student, and implemented by staff. There are few existing guidelines about how to use Social Stories. Some clinicians have also emphasized the need to evaluate how well the person with autism comprehends the content of the Social Stories.

Despite the lack of research, Social Stories are a very popular intervention. Both parents and teachers report liking Social Stories (Burke, Kuhn, & Peterson, 2004; Dodd, Hupp, Jewell, & Krohn, 2008), and often will follow recommendations to create and review Social Stories. One theory is that Social Stories might help parents and teachers pay attention to the behaviors that need improvement, which makes it more likely that they will prompt and reinforce desirable behaviors.

Rule Cards

Another visual support strategy for communication and social skills instruction is the rule card or a similar approach known as the Power Card Strategy (Gagnon, 2001). The ***Power Card*** is a small card that the child carries that summarizes a strategy to use when a particular situation arises. The card, typically the size of a business card or note card, is individualized for the child—often by including a picture of a preferred interest. Although children with autism often have limited interests, many find these interests to be extremely reinforcing. Rule Cards encourage the child to engage in the desired behavior or skill by connecting it to the special interest (Keeling, Smith Miles, Gagnon, & Simpson, 2003). For example, a card that contains reminders about how to answer questions from friends may feature a picture of the cartoon character Sponge Bob giving instructions about remembering to look at friends, listen for the question, and answer quickly.

A rule card is like a Power Card, but is generally not illustrated with a reinforcing image. The child may carry the rule card in a pocket. Alternately, the teacher may pull the card out for the child to review, post it in the classroom, or place it on a desk.

Rule cards (like Social Stories) are very easy to include in a treatment package. They are simple to use and are very similar to strategies used by parents and teachers of typically developing young children. Teachers often like the specificity and concreteness of the rule card. It simply and clearly states the behavioral expectations for a certain situation.

The sample rule cards below outline simple expectations in particular situations—eating dinner and playing. The rules are stated in very simple and clear terms. Some small social expectations are also included, such as saying "thank you" at dinner. The parameters of some rules are also reviewed. Note how trading is described as acceptable in play, if both people agree.

RULES FOR DINNER

1. Use quiet voices at the dinner table.
2. Eat what is on your plate.
3. Ask, "May I have ____, please?"
4. Say, "Thank you" when you get something.
5. When you are done, tell Mommy 1 food you liked at dinner.
6. Sit in your chair until everyone is done. Choose something to do from the activity box until dinner is over.
7. Get a reward from the treat box for following the rules!

RULES FOR PLAY

1. Choose a toy.
2. Trading is OK if both say, "Yes."
3. "NO" to trade means wait your turn.
4. When time is up, put away toy.

For children with autism who do not read, Power Cards and rule cards can be made with pictorial images or cues for the desired behavior. For example, the rules for circle time might be shown with a set of eyes ("Look at the teacher") and a picture of quiet hands ("sit quietly").

In ABA programs, the use of rule cards is generally associated with practicing a skill. For example, the teacher might review the rule card, highlight its main messages, and then contrive a situation in which the student(s) practices the skill. In this way, the teacher creates opportunities to actively and directly teach the skill. He or she can prompt the child to engage in the correct behavior. Prompts might include: telling the child exactly what to say, showing her the rule card, or simply reminding her of the rule card (either with gestures or words). Practice sessions also provide opportunities to reinforce the child for correctly demonstrating the skill.

Rule cards lend themselves readily to teaching communication skills that are important in social contexts. The following example shows how a slightly more complex skill might be depicted in a rule card and then reviewed with practice.

RULE CARD: SHARING WITH FRIENDS

When a friend asks for a turn with a toy I am using, I can say "Here" and hand the toy to my friend.

In the sample rule card above, the teacher might read the rule card, and talk about the importance of responding in a friendly way when asked to share a toy. To provide practice opportunities, she might then contrive a situation in which sharing is necessary. She may take out three scooters for four children, making it necessary for children to request turns from each other. The teacher can prompt the child without a scooter to ask a friend, and can prompt the friend to follow the rule card. At first, such assistance might take the form of actually prompting the child to say what is on the rule card ("Here") and helping the child to relinquish the item. Over time, the teacher might simply be able to remind the child of the rule.

Creating practice opportunities increases the number of instructional opportunities, which can help the child learn the skill faster. In addition, it allows the adult to elaborately praise the desired behavior, which can increase the chances that the child will use the behavior in natural contexts.

Parents can use rule cards at home to provide essential reminders for certain skills. For example, there may be a rule card for when mommy is on the telephone. (When Mommy is on the telephone, I play quietly. I wait until Mommy can talk to me. If I need to speak to her right away, I can say, "Excuse me.") Parents can orchestrate some extra practice opportunities for the rule card when teaching a new set of rules. For example, Grandma can be asked to call every hour for a few evenings.

Scripts

A closely related intervention that also directly targets communication skills is the use of scripts. A script is a cue that enables a child with autism to initiate or respond to a conversational opportunity. Sometimes written/textual scripts are used. Often, an audio script is used (via mini button recorders). Sometimes, scripts are provided via video modeling, providing both auditory, visual, and imitative cues.

In one study, Patricia Krantz and Lynn McClannahan (1998) embedded textual prompts in the activity schedules of preschoolers with autism. The schedule showed pictures of which toys to play with together with a short statement the student was to make to the teacher. Using this procedure, all the children increased their social initiations. Perhaps more importantly, the number of unscripted interactions also increased. After the instructors' instructions and cues were faded out, the children continued to initiate interactions at the same rate and generalize their interactions to new activities. Importantly, this study described an intervention that worked for young children with minimal reading skills and little social or communicative behavior.

Over the years, Drs. Krantz and McClannahan (2005) have continued to refine the use of scripts with children and teens with autism. They now define a script as "an audiotaped or written word, phrase, or sentence that enables young people with autism to start or continue conversation. The audiotaped word 'up' could be a script for a toddler; audiotaped sentences such as 'I like trucks' and 'Fire trucks are red' could be scripts for a preschooler with more language. A ten-year-old might read the typed scripts 'I go swimming on Thursdays' and 'Jan is my swimming teacher.'"

Krantz and McClannahan have developed systematic ways of prompting children to use scripts, fading the prompts, and using scripts to teach skills in:

- initiating conversation
- commenting
- extending conversations
- using the phone
- interacting with siblings and peers
- complex conversation skills

Scripts are a wonderful tool, and the audio cues are very effective for young children who are not yet reading.

Summary of Strategies to Build Social Comprehension

Communication and social skills are complicated to define, teach, and evaluate. In ABA programs, they are often targeted in a wide variety of ways, and are taught with a combination of instructional strategies. Some of the commonly used approaches include Social Stories, rule cards, scripts, and video modeling. Social Stories are probably the most widely used of these approaches, but there is the least data to support their effectiveness. As discussed above, there have been some modest reports of success, but it is not clear whether Social Stories themselves are responsible for the effects.

Video modeling and social scripting both have good empirical support. However, variability in scripts and tapes is essential to success. Rule cards may be helpful in teaching, particularly when combined with role-plays or other behavioral rehearsal techniques. (Behavioral rehearsal involves systematically practicing the components of a skill. For example, a teacher might set up a situation in which she gives markers to only three of four students in a group to create opportunities to practice asking for materials from a peer.)

To illustrate how a variety of procedures may be needed to help children with autism with their social language difficulties, let's return to the children we discussed in the last chapter and explain which strategies might help each of them.

Owen: Owen waits for people to initiate interactions with him. To help him learn to make the first move, a Social Story or rule card about talking with his friends may help, as long as there are opportunities to prompt and reinforce him for initiating interactions. He may also benefit from scripts, which could include examples of conversations that begin with him.

Doug: Doug wants to talk only about his limited interests. The best strategies for dealing with these kinds of behaviors are discussed in Chapter 8 on perseverative speech. Rule cards and Social Stories may also be helpful, especially if followed up with conversational practice. In addition, scripts on novel topics may help. Finally, video modeling or self-review of video may help Doug become more aware of his perseverative behavior and the alternatives.

Abigail: Abigail only requests preferred items. She does not easily make requests or otherwise interact with peers and adults. A few of the interventions discussed in this chapter might help expand her communication. It may be helpful to teach her joint attention skills with highly preferred items, to help bridge her into commenting on high-interest items. In addition, fill-in skills may help her begin to acquire some conversational (intraverbal) skills.

Ethan: Ethan uses PECS and cannot always communicate effectively with other children. He may benefit from watching video modeling of peer interactions, particularly in the realm of play skills. His peers may also benefit from role-plays or Social Stories about communicating via PECS.

Joshua: Joshua has slow processing speed and therefore often responds to others' interactions so slowly that they lose interest in what he has to say. He may be helped by video self-review, in which he watches and evaluates the speed of his interactive responses. Practicing his response speed may also be useful. See the section on fluency in Chapter 9 for more information on this approach.

Horatio: Horatio has trouble following rules and argues a lot. A number of the procedures discussed in this chapter may help him to better understand correct and incorrect ways of speaking with others. In particular, rule cards, Social Stories, video modeling, and self-review are all potentially useful strategies for him.

Data Collection

Generalizing skills to the natural environment is the goal of all our teaching. That is, we want children with autism to be able to use their skills in many different settings, with many different people. However, generalization is never more important than in the realm of communication and social skills.

Many of the strategies we discussed for teaching social language skills involve practicing the skills in contexts that are different from where the skill must ultimately be used. It might be practiced in a formal program, reviewed in a book, or discussed in a session introducing a rule card. Of course, the teacher is interested in how the child responds to the instruction in the moment. Teachers collect data in these teaching sessions to help them learn how to alter their instruction to make it more effective.

However, the ultimate test of instruction is whether the student learns the skill well enough to demonstrate it in the natural environment—to be able to find the words or engage in the behavior at the moment she most needs it. The success of teaching should be gauged on whether learning is transferred to these natural contexts. Does the child now return greetings in the hallway? Does she now answer a peer's questions on the playground? Does she ask for a turn on the scooter at recess?

As you probably know, data collection is *very* important for all ABA programs. Effective intervention requires regular data collection. Without objective data, we cannot tell whether the child is making meaningful progress. In addition, without data, we may continue ineffective procedures, which can lead to frustration on the child's part. Collecting data helps to ensure that the child will receive effective treatment. Of course, merely collecting data does not guarantee that instruction will be effective. Data must be analyzed on a daily basis, and adjustments in instruction must be made in response to those data.

Collecting Data during the School Day

Sometimes, parents and teachers struggle with collecting data in the natural environment. It may also be difficult to figure out how to actually assess progress with some of these social comprehension skills, because they are different from the formal teaching targets in academic skills. Below is a list of some ways in which data may be collected in the natural environment, in the context of naturally occurring social situations.

1. **Duration:** how long the child can engage in a social-communicative exchange
    - Number of conversational exchanges:
        - *This can be done with a tally of back-and-forth conversational volleys.*
    - Number of minutes in a cooperative play situation:
        - *This can be done by keeping track of start and end times.*
2. **Quality:** how well the child demonstrates a skill; that is:
    - was it appropriate?
    - was it clear?
    - was it novel (unscripted)?
        - *This can be done by tracking these qualitative elements of interaction. The instructor can code*

whether it was appropriate, understood by the other child, and novel. Alternately, the instructor can write down the content of what the child said, and code it later for these qualities.

3. **Independence:** how independently the child demonstrates a skill:
   - Did she need help to engage in the correct behavior?
   - What kind of help did she need?
     - ❑ *This can be tracked by separately (but simultaneously) collecting data on independent vs. prompted responses. (You might tally the independent and prompted responses separately in two columns, or you might use two different golf counters.) A very simple way to track responses would be to use two counting clickers that are labeled "Independent" and "Prompted." You can easily carry these around with you by hooking them onto your belt, purse, or bag. Depending on how long you want to track data, you can collect for an hour, a few hours, or an entire day.*
     - *It is an index of progress to see the child make more independent and fewer prompted responses over time. In addition, it is often helpful to track the type of prompt given. Did she need to be fed the lines to say (scripting) or simply need to be reminded to answer?*
4. **Percent of opportunity:** what percentage of the time that the child *could* have demonstrated the skill *did* he or she demonstrate the skill?
     - ❑ *This can be tracked by tallying the opportunities as they occur and indicating whether the child responded as desired. In other words, another child may approach her 5 times on the playground and ask her to join an activity. Of those 5 times, she may independently respond to the peer on 4 occasions. This would be 80% of the opportunities.*

Of course, several of these strategies can also be combined. Teachers might want information about duration and level of independence in conversation. Or they may want information about both percent of opportunity that the child engaged in the behavior and some qualitative index of her response. (Was it audible? Was it combined with eye contact?) All of these elements of the response might be important qualitative aspects that influence the success of the interaction, and can be evaluated objectively and tracked systematically.

Collecting Data at Home

Parents may collect data in the home for many reasons. Sometimes ongoing data collection provides a way for you to track your child's progress in the development of a skill. Other times, you may collect data on how well your child has transferred a new skill to the home, to ensure that she has generalized the skill. You may also collect data in natural contexts that arise, to ensure that the skill targeted and taught now happens when and where it needs to (e.g., does your child ask to use the restroom when out in the community?).

Generally, it is harder to collect data at home than at school. It is simply more difficult for parents in busy home environments to remember to collect data and to balance data collection with other demands. Often, parents adapt by collecting data less frequently. For example, you might do weekly probes to check on your child's progress. Another family member or instructor could do this instead of you as well, which can make your interactions more natural.

Whenever you do collect data, it is important that you treat the behavior the same as you do at other times. For example, do not provide extra help so that your child passes a probe. Data are always most valuable when they provide a real-life, realistic snapshot of what your child actually does in the natural environment. For more information on collecting data at home, you may wish to refer to the chapter on "Evaluating What You Are Doing" in the book *Autism 24/7* by Andy Bondy and Lori Frost.

References

Baker, J. E. (2003a). *Social Skills Training*. Shawnee Mission, KS: Autism Asperger Publishing Co.

Baker, J. E. (2003b). *Social Skills Picture Book: Teaching Play, Emotion, and Communication to Children with Autism.* Arlington, TX: Future Horizons.

Barry, L. M. & Burlew, S. B. (2004). Using social stories to teach choice and play skills to children with autism. *Focus on Autism and Other Developmental Disabilities 19*, 45–51.

Bondy, A. and Frost, L. (2008). *Autism 24/7: A Family Guide to Learning at Home and in the Community.* Bethesda, MD: Woodbine House.

Brownell, M. D. (2002). Musically adapted social stories to modify behaviors in students with autism: Four case studies. *Journal of Music Therapy 39,* 117-44.

Bruinsma, Y., Koegel, R. L., & Koegel, L. K. (2004). Joint attention and children with autism: A review of the literature. *Mental Retardation and Developmental Disorders 10,* 169-75.

Buggey, T. (2009). *Seeing Is Believing: Video Self-Modeling for People with Autism and Other Developmental Disabilities.* Bethesda, MD: Woodbine House.

Burke, R. V., Kuhn, B. R., & Peterson, J. L. (2004.) Brief report: A storybook ending to children's bedtime problems—the use of a rewarding social story to reduce bedtime resistance and frequent night waking. *Journal of Pediatric Psychology 29,* 389-96.

Charlop, M. H. & Milstein, J. P. (1989). Teaching autistic children conversational speech using video modeling. *Journal of Applied Behavior Analysis 22*, 275-85.

Charlop-Christy, M. H., Le, L., & Freeman, K. A. (2000). A comparison of video modeling with in vivo modeling for teaching children with autism. *Journal of Autism and Developmental Disorders 30*, 537-52.

Crozier, S. & Tincani, M. (2007). Effects of social stories on prosocial behavior of preschool children with autism spectrum disorders. *Journal of Autism and Developmental Disorders 37,* 1803-1814.

Dodd, S., Hupp, S. D. A., Jewell, J. D., & Krohn, E. (2008). Using parents and siblings during a social story intervention for two children diagnosed with PDD-NOS. *Journal of Developmental and Physical Disabilities 20*, 217-29.

Dowrick, P.W. (1983). Self-modeling. In P.W. Dowrick & J. Biggs (Eds.), *Using Video: Psychological and Social Applications* (pp. 105-24). New York, NY: Wiley.

Gray, C. A. (1995). Teaching children with autism to 'read' social situations. In K. A. Quill (Ed.), *Teaching Children with Autism; Strategies to Enhance Communication and Socialization* (pp. 219-42). Albany, NY: Delmar Pub.

Gray, C. (2000). How to write a Social Story. *The New Social Story Handbook* (illustrated edition). Arlington, TX: Future Horizons.

Gray, C. (1993). *The Original Social Story Book*. Arlington, TX: Future Horizons.

Gray, C. (1994). *The New Social Story Book*. Arlington, TX: Future Horizons.

Haring, T., Kennedy, C., Adams, M., & Pitts-Conway, V. (1987). Teaching generalization of purchasing skills across community settings to autistic youth using videotape modeling. *Journal of Applied Behavior Analysis 20,* 89-96.

Kasari, C., Freeman, S. & Paparella, T. (2006). Joint attention and symbolic play in young children with autism: A randomized controlled intervention study. *Journal of Child Psychology and Psychiatry 47(6),* 611-20.

Kasari, C., Paparella, T., Freeman, S., & Jahromi, L.B. (2008). Language outcome in autism: Randomized comparison of joint attention and play interventions. *Journal of Consulting and Clinical Psychology 76(1),* 125-37.

Krantz, P. J ., MacDuff, G., S., Wadstrom, O., & McClannahan, L. E. (1991). Using video with developmentally disabled learners In P. W. Dowrick (Ed.), *Practical Guide to Video in the Behavioral Sciences* (256-66). New York, NY: John Wiley & Sons.

Krantz, P. J. & McClannahan, L. E. (1993). Teaching children with autism to initiate to peers: Effects of a script-fading procedure. *Journal of Applied Behavior Analysis 26*, 121-32.

McClannahan, L. E. & Krantz, P. J. (2005). *Teaching Conversation to Children with Autism: Scripts and Script Fading.* Bethesda, MD: Woodbine House.

McGinnis, E. & Goldstein, A. P. (1990). *Skillstreaming.* Champaign, IL: Research Press.

Morales, M., Mundy, P., Delgado, C. E. F., Yale, M., Messinger, D., Neal, R. & Schwartz, H. K. (2000). Responding to joint attention across the 6- through 24-month age period and early language acquisition. *Journal of Applied Developmental Psychology 21 (3),* 283-98.

More, C. (2008). Digital stories targeting social skills for children with disabilities: Multidimensional learning. *Intervention in School and Clinic 43,* 168-77.

Mundy, P., Block, J., Vaughan Van Hecke, A., Delgadoa, C., Venezia Parlade, M. & Pomares, Y. (2007). Individual differences and the development of infant joint attention. *Child Development 78* (3), 938-54.

Mundy, P. & Crawson, M. (1997). Joint attention and early social communication implications for research on intervention with autism. *Journal of Autism and Developmental Disorders 27,* 653-76.

Reynhout, G. & Carter, M. (2006). Social stories for children with disabilities. *Journal of Autism and Developmental Disorders 36*, 445-69.

Richardson, R. C. (1996). *Connecting with Others: Lessons for Teaching Social and Emotional Competence*. Champaign, IL: Research Press.

Rogers, S. J. (2000). Interventions that facilitate socialization in children with autism. *Journal of Autism and Developmental Disorders 30* (5), 399–409.

Sansosti, F. J. & Powell-Smith, K. A. (2008). Using computer-presented social stories and video models to increase the social communication skills of children with high-functioning autism spectrum disorders. *Journal of Positive Behavior Interventions 10,* 162-78.

Sheinkopf, S. J., Mundy, P., Claussen, A. H., & Willoughby, J. (2004). Infant joint attention skill and preschool behavioral outcomes in at-risk children. *Development and Psychopathology 16,* 273-91.

Sherer, M. , Pierce, K. L., Parades, S., Kisacky, K. L., Ingersoll, B., & Schreibman, L. (2001). Enhancing conversation skills in children with autism via video technology: Which is better, "self" or "other" as a model. *Behavior Modification 25,* 140-58.

Snell, M. E. & Brown, F. (2000). *Instruction of Students with Severe Handicaps.* Upper Saddle River, NJ: Prentice Hall.

Swaggart, B. L., Gagnon, E., Bock, S. J., Earles, T. L., Quinn, C., Myles, B. S. et al. (1995). Using social stories to teach social and behavioral skills to children with autism. *Focus on Autistic Behavior 10,* 1–16.

Taylor, B. (2009). Improving joint attention and reciprocal language skills in children with autism. Invited presenter summary article from ABAI Autism Conference in Jacksonville, Florida. *Association for Behavior Analysis International Newsletter.* Spring 2009 issue.

Taylor, B. A. (2001). Teaching peer social skills to children with autism. In C. Maurice, G. Green, & R. Foxx (Eds.), *Making a Difference: Behavioral Intervention for Autism* (pp. 83-96). Austin, TX: Pro-Ed.

Taylor, B. A., & Hoch, H. (2008). Teaching children with autism to respond to and to initiate bids for joint attention. *Journal of Applied Behavior Analysis* 41, 377-91.

Taylor, B. A. & Jasper, S. (2001). Teaching programs to increase peer interaction. In C. Maurice, G. Green, & R. Foxx (Eds.), *Making a Difference: Behavioral Intervention for Autism* (pp. 97-162). Austin, TX: Pro-Ed.

Thiemann, K. S. & Goldstein, H. (2001). Social stories, written text cues, and video feedback: Effects on social communication of children with autism. *Journal of Applied Behavior Analysis 34,* 425-46.

Vismara, L.A. & Lyons, G.L. (2007). Using perseverative interests to elicit joint attention behaviors in young children with autism: Theoretical and clinical implications for understanding motivation. *Journal of Positive Behavioral Interventions 9 (4)*, 214-228.

Watkins, L. T., Sprafkin, J. N. & Krolikowski, D. M. (1993). Using videotaped lessons to facilitate the development of manual sign skills in students with mental retardation. *Augmentative and Alternative Communication 9*, 177-83.

Weiss, M. J. & Harris, S. L. (2001). *Reaching Out, Joining In: Teaching Social Skills to Young Children with Autism*. Bethesda, MD: Woodbine House.

Whalen, C. & Schreibman, L. (2003). Joint attention training for children using behavior modification procedures. *Journal of Child Psychiatry 44*, 456-68.

7 Humming, Screeching, and Other Repetitive Sounds: Understanding and Reducing Perseverative Vocalizations

Ideally, the goal for all children with autism spectrum disorders is to communicate effectively through speech, which is why most of this book focuses on ways to encourage speech skills. Sometimes, however, children with ASD make vocalizations that are problematic.

Many children with autism engage in vocalizations that are not communicative and that interfere with their ability to socialize and participate in activities at school and in the community. These kinds of vocal stereotypy behaviors include humming and making nonspeech noises. (A stereotypy is a repetitive behavior that does not seem to serve a useful function.) Many other children with ASD exhibit another kind of repetitive nonfunctional speech—they become obsessed with certain topics and want to speak about these topics incessantly.

These types of stereotypical vocalizations are not always a high priority for intervention (compared with aggressive or destructive behaviors). Still, it is often in the child's best interest to intervene and try to reduce or eliminate the behavior. This chapter explains how to decide whether to try to intervene and explains the behavioral methods that may be used to reduce nonspeech vocal stereotypies such as humming and screeching. The next chapter addresses repetitive speech and echolalia.

Why Intervene?

Stereotypical vocalizations are usually very self-reinforcing, or automatically reinforcing. That is, children who engage in these behaviors often do it because they like to. They may enjoy the sensory feedback they get from hearing their own voices. Often, these behaviors strengthen over time simply because they are so enjoyable for the child. Without intervention, the vocalizations can increasingly interfere with learning and other activities. Indeed, stereotypy is not likely to decrease without intervention (Horner, Carr, Strain, Todd, & Reed, 2002; Jones, 1999; Oliver 1995).

Several studies have shown that stereotypical behavior often interferes with skill acquisition (Dunlap, Dyer, & Koegel, 1983; Koegel and Covert, 1972; Morrison & Rosales-Ruiz, 1997; Nijhof et al., 1998). Often children who make these vocalizations are simply not available for instruction. They frequently tune out instructions or others' attempts to interact with them, and simply entertain themselves. Such behaviors absolutely make it harder for them to be meaningfully engaged in instruction or social interactions.

Finally, studies have also suggested that stereotypical behavior is stigmatizing and may interfere with the development of social behavior and relationships (Jones, Wint, & Ellis, 1990). It is certainly true that such behaviors can be off-putting. The behaviors may look and sound odd to others, so that peers and adults may be less likely to interact with the child. Reducing the child's stereotypic behaviors can make it easier and more rewarding for others to interact with him.

If your child has perseverative vocalizations that interfere with socialization and participation in instruction, his team will probably choose to treat these behaviors. Intervention can be extremely important, especially given the likelihood that the behaviors will persist and may worsen without appropriate intervention.

How Much Stereotypy Is Too Much?

With stereotypical vocalizations, as with other problematic behaviors, it is important to pick your battles. That is, you must choose your goal wisely and ensure that the effort needed to reach the goal is worth it. With some behaviors such as aggression, complete elimination of the behavior is the goal. Such a goal makes sense for many behaviors, especially since many school systems have a zero tolerance policy for aggressive behavior or threats.

However, with perseverative and stereotypical behaviors, elimination is not necessarily (or realistically) the goal. Sometimes a successful intervention for stereotypy might mean that the child still subtly engages in the behavior from time to time. Whether a behavior should be completely eliminated depends on the extent and form of the stereotypy. More severe and disruptive behaviors are associated with more negative social consequences.

In fact, most of us engage in some stereotypical behaviors. (Do you bite your fingernails? Twirl your hair?) Young typically developing children have many behaviors similar to those we see in excess in children with autism. Of course, in typically developing children, these behaviors usually occur briefly and infrequently, and do not pose challenges to attending, learning, or group participation. However, it is sometimes helpful to observe typically developing children to help gauge how different a child with autism appears in that setting. Ask yourself: To what extent do the child's behaviors exceed those of his typically developing peers? Do the typically developing peers have behaviors that are similar? This may provide some information about forms of the behavior that could be more socially acceptable and less stigmatizing.

Sometimes it is possible to shape the form of the behavior into something more socially acceptable. For example, a child who was screeching might learn to hum briefly at a nearly inaudible level. However, this goal must be approached with caution, in light of all of the other things we have said about stereotypy. Even a subtle form of the behavior could interfere with learning and set the child socially apart from his peers.

The following list of questions can help guide parents and teachers in deciding whether to intervene and whether elimination of the behavior is essential:

- Does the behavior interfere with learning?
- Is the behavior disruptive to others?
- Do other children seem bothered by the behavior?
- Does the behavior look or sound odd?
- Is it easy to redirect the behavior?
- Is it getting worse?

If you answer "yes" to at least one question, it may be wise to intervene.

Why Do Children with Autism Perseverate?

Intervening to reduce stereotypical vocalizations is not always so easy. One of the first tasks is to understand more about how and why the child with autism is engaging in this behavior. It is important to understand as much as possible about the behavior before planning a treatment approach. Generally, there are two factors to consider when trying to understand the underlying causes:

1. What is going on in the child's environment when he is engaging in vocal perseveration?
2. What does the child get out of the behavior that encourages him to keep doing it?

Often when a child with autism is making repetitive speech sounds it is because something is happening (or not happening) in his immediate environment. Stereotypical behavior can occur during periods of low stimulation and "over-stimulation" (Repp, Karsh, Deitz, & Singh, 1992). In other words, stereotypical behavior is most likely to occur either when the child feels as if he doesn't have many other options for behavior (and may be bored or under-stimulated) *or* when he feels as if there is too much stimulation (Hall, Thorns, & Oliver, 2003; Lovaas, Newsom, & Hickman, 1987; Michael, 1993; Laraway, 2003).

As mentioned above, stereotypical behaviors may also occur because they are self-reinforcing or automatically reinforcing. The child enjoys making the sounds and they serve a useful function for him. Sometimes the behavior can also serve social purposes (Kennedy, Meyer, Knowles, & Shukla, 2000). This may be particularly the case when a child talks excessively (perseverates) on a particular topic.

Even if the behavior initially only occurs for automatically reinforcing reasons, the child may discover other purposes. Such discoveries are often quite accidental, but can lead to the child using the behavior in additional situations. For example, classmates may walk away from the child with autism if he hums loudly. For a child who is anxious and avoids social interaction, this may be a bonus. It might lead to more humming as a way to keep peers away. A child may also continue to engage in stereotypical behavior if he learns it can help him gain access to sensory activities (e.g., preferred motor activities that are provided as distractions), tangible items (e.g., toys that provide sensory input), or attention.

In general, it is important to understand as much as we can about the functions of behavior so that we can intervene effectively. This may require doing a functional behavior assessment if the function of the behavior is not readily apparent (see box). When we understand why a child is engaging in a behavior, we can develop a plan to reduce the likelihood that the behavior will occur. In many cases, we can make changes in the environment to help reduce the occurrence of the behavior. For example, it might be possible to alter levels of stimulation or other aspects of the setting.

Behavioral Treatments: Changing the Environment

If a child's perseverative vocalizations are related to an under- or over-stimulating environment, you can often make changes to the environment that will help reduce the problematic behavior. If the child

What Is a Functional Behavior Assessment?

The purpose of a functional behavior assessment (FBA) is to identify *why* a child may be engaging in a particular behavior. We no longer think of behaviors as happening in a vacuum; we know that behaviors happen for a reason. It follows, then, that if a problematic behavior persists, it is working for a child in some way. In other words, some need is being met through the behavior. Often, the behaviors of children with autism serve a communicative function. We need to understand what the child needs and what the behavior is communicating. When we do, we can intervene effectively.

Possible Functions: Four main functions of behavior have been identified: attention, escape, tangible, and automatic.

A child engages in attention-motivated behaviors because they result in attention. For example, he may use perseverative speech because it attracts his peers' attention. Escape-motivated behaviors persist because they have been successful in disrupting, avoiding, or delaying demands. Again, perseverative speech may help a child delay a task that he does not want to participate in. Tangible-motivated behaviors result in the person receiving access to specific items or activities that he wants. Once again, this might be a reason for using perseverative speech—for example, if the child has learned he will be allowed to use the computer to calm down his perseverative speech. Automatically reinforcing behaviors persist because of the sensory consequences that result from the behaviors. The individual simply enjoys engaging in the behavior, and it occurs independent of any social context or consequence.

is bored or under-stimulated, you can take steps to make his environment more interesting or enriching. If the child is over-stimulated, you can limit the sources of stimulation in the environment, systematically increase the amount of time the child spends in the environment between strategic breaks, or teach him to ask for a break when there is too much stimulation.

If the Child Is Under-stimulated

Environmental enrichment can be an effective treatment for children who use vocalizations when they are under-stimulated. Essentially, you give the child access to highly preferred items in hopes that he would rather use these items than amuse himself with vocalizations. Numerous studies have demonstrated that simply providing different sources of reinforcement in the form of preferred items is effective at reducing stereotypy (e.g., Mueller & Kafka, 2006; Piazza, Adelinis, Hanley, Goh, & Delia, 2000; Ringdahl, Vollmer, Marcus, & Roane, 1997; Vollmer et al., 1994).

Some children become easily bored. In this case, it may be necessary to continually vary items and activities available and work to identify new items they prefer. Other children highly prefer only a few items, and it is important to provide just those items. In all cases, it is important to use good behavioral teaching to ensure that the child does not learn to engage in the behaviors in order to get access to the preferred item. In other words, these items should be provided *before* or *independent* of the actual problem behavior.

Some researchers have found that it can help to provide reinforcing items and activities that provide similar sensory consequences as the stereotypy (e.g., Higbee, Chang, & Endicott, 2005; Piazza et al., 2000; Roberts-Gwynn, Luiten, Derby, Johnson, & Weber, 2001; Sidener, Carr, & Firth, 2005, Tang, Patterson, & Kennedy, 2003). For example, if your child craves auditory stimulation, giving him a radio to listen to may help reduce his vocal stereotypy.

For children who seem to be motivated to receive auditory feedback, it may help to explore different ways of providing that feedback, as some of these alternatives may be much more preferable to the child. Think about the toys that you have in your home or classroom. There are vehicles that make sounds, See 'n Say toys with animal sounds, toys that play songs, books with sounds, etc. In addition, there are many different kinds of music and a wide array of books on tape or e-books. A behavior analyst can conduct a functional analysis to help determine exactly which types of feedback are most effective in reducing your child's perseverative behaviors. Perhaps certain kinds of music work better for him, or perhaps he prefers white noise or tapes of himself vocalizing.

Possible sensory consequences go beyond auditory feedback. If a child grinds his teeth, it may not be because he enjoys the sound. He may like the sensation or the pressure. In this case, chewing on gum or eating hard pretzels, licorice, or taffy may provide similar sensory input. Similarly, a child may buzz his lips for the funny sensation, not for the sound *per se.* In this case, an alternative to try might be a vibrating toy that can be placed on the lips. A preschooler may squint his eyes and yell into his hand for a combination of auditory and visual sensations. Toys that produce both lights and noises may compete with this behavior.

The issue of matching the sensory consequence is not entirely understood. Opinions vary, data have been mixed, and consensus has yet to be achieved. It is widely agreed, though, that access to preferred items can reduce stereotypy. This may be because the child has alternatives in an enriched environment, and will select other options rather than engaging in stereotypic vocalizations.

Sometimes it is not enough to just provide a child with access to alternative items. He may need prompting or reminding to use the items in place of making vocalizations. A few studies have shown that periodically reminding the child to use the alternative items is effective at reducing stereotypy (e.g., Britton et al., 2002). If you need to remind your child to play with or use the item that is designed to compete with the behavior, use frequently calm reminders throughout the day—not just in response to his vocalizations. Giving your child additional reinforcement when he appropriately interacts with the items can also increase the effectiveness of the treatment (e.g., Favell, McGimsey, & Schell, 1982; Vollmer et al., 1994). So, if your child plays with a remote control car for a number of minutes and does not screech while he's playing, you can give him a bonus reinforcement. Ideally, this might include extra time with the car, but it could include a particular snack, a tickle, or anything else that is reinforcing to him.

To summarize, the most important step in preventing vocal stereotypy due to under-stimulation is to make alternative activities and items readily available to the child. It may be especially helpful to make sure that some of these items provide similar kinds of sensory feedback to the child as the perseverative behavior provides. In the case of perseverative vocalizations, the feedback is likely to be auditory. However, it could provide other sensory consequences as well, such as tactile feedback, as in the case of lip buzzing.

Sometimes it may be necessary to help the child learn to seek out alternative forms of stimulation. The main strategies involve providing prompts and reinforcement to help your child do so.

Ways to provide reminders include:

- visual cues (e.g., a picture of your child playing with toys),
- drawing your child's attention to toys available,
- modeling playing with toys,
- verbally instructing your child to play with toys.

Ways to provide reinforcement include:

- verbal praise,
- nonverbal praise (e.g., thumbs up, high five, smile),
- tokens,
- point systems.

If the Child Is Over-stimulated

When a child hums, screeches, or engages in other vocalizations because he is over-stimulated by sensations in his environment, intervention generally focuses on: 1) reducing his exposure to those sensations, but also 2) teaching him to gradually tolerate more of the sensations that he has trouble dealing with.

Limiting Sources of Stimulation: All children must eventually learn to adapt to noise and other stimuli in their environments. While they are learning, however, it is sometimes wise to provide them with strategies to reduce their exposure to bothersome stimuli. Some ways to limit a child's exposure to stimulation that leads to vocalizations include:

- noise blocking headphones,
- white noise,
- blocking specific sources of noise (e.g., putting tennis balls on chair legs that screech when pushed back or using rugs or carpets to deaden sounds),
- strategic seating away from loud students or annoying sounds such as the air conditioner,

- reducing visual overstimulation by simplifying the classroom environment (removing clutter) or providing a work setting without visual distractions.

Teaching Tolerance: Children need to be able to tolerate the sensations that annoy or upset them, and procedures can be developed to build this tolerance. Just as with other skills, we can systematically approach the task and gradually build the child's capacity. We may begin by having the child spend just a minute in a loud environment, for example. When he can tolerate this amount of time, we may try one and a half minutes, two minutes, three minutes, five minutes, etc.

We can also equip the child with skills that allow him to cope more effectively with sights, sounds, and other sensations. For example, we can provide him with a "break" or "exit" card to give to a teacher or parent when he wants to escape an annoying noise. This procedure can work even with children who do not speak or who cannot effectively communicate when upset.

Combining an exit strategy with a plan to build tolerance for the nonpreferred stimuli can effectively address many children's problems with over-stimulation.

John: Enriching the Environment to Reduce Vocalizations

The case story that follows illustrates how some of the techniques introduced above might be used to help a young child on the autism spectrum reduce his vocal stereotypy.

John is a two-year-old boy with PDD who was beginning to learn foundation skills in his ABA program. While he was beginning to make some progress, he also had behaviors that interfered with his ability to learn, attend, and respond to instruction. He engaged in a great deal of vocal stereotypy, most notably humming and making a loud screeching "eee" sound. These vocalizations were increasing, even though he had adjusted well overall to structured ABA intervention. A functional assessment indicated that John engaged in the behavior for automatically reinforcing reasons—he liked to make these sounds.

It was quite difficult to get John to stop humming and screeching. Even when John's teachers tried to get John to verbally imitate sounds or words instead of screeching or humming, he often imitated *and* screeched or hummed. John's teachers did notice that his humming was worse during unstructured times, and thought that it might be a way he entertained himself. They decided to try to enrich his environment with some toys that provided interesting auditory feedback.

John's team conducted preference assessments to determine what toys and other sources of auditory stimulation he enjoyed. At first, they just provided John with a wide variety of toys and activities in a free play situation. This helped them identify items in the natural environment that he was drawn to. However, it did not give enough information about the types of auditory stimulation that might be especially interesting to him.

They decided to do more ***formal preference assessments,*** focused on items and activities that could provide unique sources of auditory stimulation. The team thought that this information might be especially important, because John used his hums and screeches for automatic reinforcement. If they could understand exactly what he enjoyed about the sounds, they might be able to identify a source of auditory stimulation that could compete with the stereotypy, and maybe even replace it.

In one kind of preference assessment, they presented John with a choice of two different toys. In this assessment, they got information about his relative preferences. In another kind of assessment, they presented John with an array of toys, and had John choose one item. When he was done with that item, they presented him with the rest of the array (i.e., the remaining items except for the one(s) he had already sampled). At the end of this assessment, they had information not just about preferences and comparisons, but also about hierarchies of preferred items.

John's team found that he really liked certain kinds of toys, including See 'n Says and a toy piano. In addition, they taught him to wear headphones. They had him listen to his favorite music, many other different types of music, his favorite books on tape, and sounds of himself humming. They eventually included these items/tapes in the array of items available to him.

When John was given free access to these items during unstructured times of the day, his vocal stereotypy decreased significantly. When he didn't have access to the items, he engaged in vocal stereotypy in 80 percent of one-minute intervals. (See the section on "Logistical Challenges," below, for information on data collection methods.) John's vocalizations dropped to only 24 percent of one-minute intervals when he did have access to his preferred items. Next, John's team began to prompt him to use the toys. With periodic reminders, his vocal stereotypy reduced so he was only humming or screeching in 15 percent of one-minute intervals. The improvement in John's behavior can be seen in the graph below.

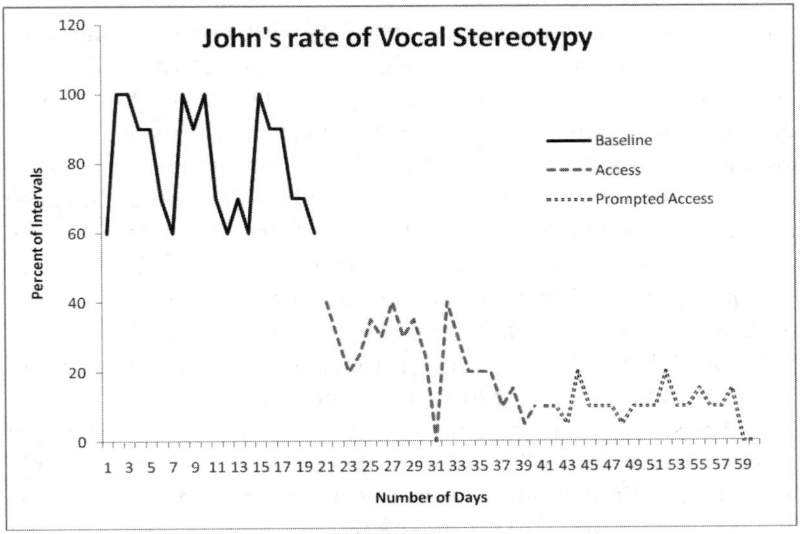

The team also wanted to know more specifically which kinds of auditory stimulation were working best. Although it was clear that they had been successful in competing with the behavior, they wanted to increase their efficiency and identify strategies that would be effective in every situation (e.g., when John was out in the community).

John's team decided to do a functional analysis to determine which kind of stimulation was most effective in reducing his vocalizations. They had John listen to different kinds of auditory input in five-minute segments, and recorded his rate of stereotypy. The specific stimuli assessed included:

- preferred music,
- random music,
- favorite auditory toys,
- white noise,
- Dr. Seuss books on tape, and
- recordings of John's vocalizations.

They found that John vocalized the least when he listened to books on tape or to his own vocalizations. This made it easier to reduce the array of choices, and to decide upon good choices to make available for trips into the community.

Later in intervention, John's team tackled the problem of reducing his auditory over-stimulation. In many situations, it was perfectly acceptable for John to wear headphones, including during some times at school. (In other words, if it did not interfere with John's learning and it reduced his humming and screeching, the team allowed him to listen to headphones.) However, it was not acceptable for him to wear headphones during group learning activities. Furthermore, it made him less socially available to peers when he wore headphones during free play time.

The team developed two strategies to help decrease John's need for auditory stimulation. The first involved implementing a waiting program. If John asked to use the headphones, he was told, "Yes, but you have to wait." They then set a visual timer for a brief period of time, which allowed John to track how quickly he would have access to the headphones. Initially, they set the timer for just one minute, but eventually they worked up to a ten-minute wait time.

The second strategy required more self-control from John, and was not introduced until he was four years old. As he became better at waiting, they limited the number of requests for headphones that he had available for the day. They did this by providing him with cards that he could trade in for a session with the headphones. At first, they gave him twenty cards, which was about his daily average of requests. Over time, they reduced the number of cards systematically, until he had just five headphone request cards. The team increased their expectations for John only when he was succeeding in the program—maintaining low rates of humming and screeching and requesting the headphones at or below the targeted level.

Behavioral Treatments: Providing Consequences

Besides changing the environment if it is over- or under-stimulating, the other main strategy for reducing perseverative vocalizations is to change the consequences that occur when the child does or does not engage in the behavior. The goal is to make the consequences of *not* vocalizing more rewarding than vocalizing. In ABA programs, the main ways of accomplishing this are through:

- reinforcement procedures, or
- sensory extinction procedures.

Differential Reinforcement Procedures

Various forms of a procedure known as differential reinforcement can be used to reduce a child's stereotypical behaviors. During differential reinforcement, the child may receive a reinforcer for:

- the absence of the behavior for a set time interval (differential reinforcement of other behavior; DRO);
- an alternative behavior such as a request for a different sensory item (differential reinforcement of alternative behavior; DRA);
- instances of the behavior that occur after a period with no stereotypy (differential reinforcement of low-rate behavior; DRL).

To use any of these procedures, you need to come up with a variety of items or activities that the child finds rewarding. The exact ways in which the rewards are used differ, depending on the individual. For some children, it works best to explain the entire procedure in advance, as a series of rules associated with rewards. For other children, it works better if reinforcers are provided without such an elaborate explanation. The procedures can work in a variety of different ways, depending on the child's characteristics, developmental level, and compliance.

Bear in mind that it isn't always necessary to completely eliminate the problematic vocalizations. For example, if the noise isn't too distracting for others or if the child only makes it during certain times of the day or in certain settings, it may be all right for him to occasionally vocalize. In these situations, a DRL schedule may be an appropriate treatment option. The steps to follow in using this strategy include:

1. identifying the current rate of the behavior;
2. identifying the goal rate;
3. identifying sequential goals for reduction.

For example, a child may hum every 4 minutes. The team may wish to reduce the behavior to every 20 minutes. They may begin by rewarding the child for engaging in the behavior every 4 minutes OR LESS FREQUENTLY, then every 6 minutes OR LESS FREQUENTLY, then every 8 minutes or less, then every 10 minutes or less, then every 15 minutes or less, etc.

Whatever treatment method is chosen, it can be challenging to treat these behaviors consistently all day long. Consequently, if a child is still vocalizing frequently, treatment may be done for just a portion of the day (e.g., during two one-hour 1:1 work sessions). As the behavior becomes more manageable, the plan may then be extended across the day.

For more detailed information on specific reinforcement procedures, you may wish to refer to *Incentives for Change: Motivating People with Autism Spectrum Disorders to Learn and Gain Independence* (Delmolino & Harris, 2004).

Billy: Reducing Vocalizations through DRO

Billy, age three, hummed softly but almost continually. He was very new to ABA instruction and had not yet mastered basic skills. He was also extremely noncompliant. His team spent most of their time with him trying to increase his compliance. They provided many rewards for following the simplest of requests.

Billy's team knew that his humming would interfere with his attention and his ability to respond to directions. However, they were reluctant to intervene in a significant way, given how fragile their rapport with him was, how much work needed to be done in all areas, and Billy's newness to intervention. They decide that the simplest intervention would be to reinforce him for short periods when he did not hum during the interval. (This is Differential Reinforcement of Other Behavior, since he was rewarded as long as he was not humming.)

Since Billy hummed so frequently, it was difficult for the team to decide on how to implement the procedure. Given that Billy hummed in 100 percent of 5-minute intervals, 60 percent of 1-minute intervals, and 40 percent of 30-second intervals, they decided to intervene on a 30-second schedule. They chose this interval because it ensured success. They would have lots of opportunities to reinforce Billy if they began with such a rich schedule. In addition, it would increase the learning opportunities for Billy.

However, there were inherent difficulties in reinforcing Billy so frequently. It wasn't really possible to keep up that level of vigilance and availability of staff throughout the day. Instead, the team implemented the plan for two one-hour periods of the day. This ensured that they were able to consistently reinforce Billy. They developed criteria for expanding the length of the interval, and also for extending the plan into other segments of his day. They decided that they would not extend the plan beyond the two one-hour sessions until Billy could go for ten minutes without humming.

The procedure was very successful at reducing Billy's humming. Over time, he went from almost continual humming to humming in less than 10 percent of 10-minute intervals.

Kyle: Reducing Vocalizations and Increasing Speech Sounds through DRA

Kyle was identified early as being at risk for autism because he has an older brother with autism. His parents and pediatrician watched him very closely, and he began receiving early intervention services before he turned one year old.

At twenty months, Kyle had yet to develop effective vocal communication, although he was learning to communicate via PECS. His team was very concerned about the subtle but very consistent noises he made. He kept up an almost constant stream of soft sounds, most of which did not resemble speech. The team feared that these vocalizations interfered with his ability to attend to them and to acquire skills. Their data showed that he rarely responded correctly if he was vocalizing. This was true for nonvocal responses as well as for vocal responses. For example, Kyle was unlikely to clap his hands imitatively or wave goodbye to his teacher at the end of the day if he was making noises at the same time.

The team was afraid that Kyle would make fewer vocal sounds, however, if they focused on the noises he was making. In particular, they feared that he might stop vocally imitating. Consequently, they decided to address the issue by giving Kyle higher quality reinforcers when he responded to instructions without making vocalizations. When he quietly imitated his teachers, he received highly prized tangible rewards such as gummy bears and being thrown in the air. However, when his responses were accompanied by vocal stereotypy, he simply received verbal praise.

In this way, Kyle's teachers differentially reinforced higher quality responses. Responses that were communicative and did not contain the other sounds were rewarded with favored items and activities; responses accompanied by other sounds were not. Over time, Kyle began to make many more responses without the vocal noises. His rate of skill acquisition also increased, as he was more often successful when he was attending better to instruction.

When Behavior Is Motivated by Sensory Consequences

As discussed above, stereotypic behaviors often occur because the child enjoys the sensory consequences associated with them. Sensory extinction involves preventing or reducing these sensory consequences. Several studies have investigated the effects of sensory extinction on stereotypy (e.g., Rapp, Dozier, et al., 2000; Rapp, Miltenberger, Galensky, Ellingson, & Long, 1999; Rapp, Miltenberger, et al., 2000; Rincover, 1978). These studies suggest that sensory extinction works when it is specifically tailored to the target behavior. When using sensory extinction, it is important to know exactly which sensory aspects of the behavior are reinforcing to the child.

One way to prevent or reduce sensory consequences is to use a strategy called ***response blocking*** or ***response interruption.*** These procedures prevent the child from engaging in stereotypic behavior through physically blocking the response (e.g., guiding his hands down when he flaps them) or ensuring that he makes an incompatible response (e.g., prompting him to say the appropriate word instead of engaging in vocal stereotypy).

It is considerably more difficult to block, redirect, or interrupt vocal stereotypies (compared to motor stereotypies.) Some children simply resist stopping the behavior. Others respond to the prompt/redirection, but still engage in the stereotypy. For example, they might answer a simple question in the midst of continuing to hum. That is, they simply mix in the correct response to the redirection with inappropriate vocalizations.

Despite those logistical challenges, it can be very helpful and effective to interrupt, redirect, or prevent vocalizations. Using response blocking/interruption alone and in conjunction with other treatments has been found to be highly effective at reducing rates of stereotypy (Ahearn, Clark, MacDonald, & Chung, 2007; Athens, Vollmer, Sloman, & Pipkin, 2008; Hagopian & Toole, 2009).

In one recent study, several researchers evaluated a response interruption and redirection (RIRD) procedure in the treatment of vocal stereotypy with two children (Ahearn et al., 2007). During RIRD, the therapist prompted the children to make an alternative vocal response (vocal imitation) each time vocal stereotypy occurred. This procedure decreased both children's stereotypic vocalizations and increased one child's appropriate vocalizations.

Matthew: Response Interruption/Redirection

Matthew, a three-year-old with autism, frequently screeched and screamed, in many different situations. The function of his behavior appeared to be mainly automatic reinforcement, though it also garnered attention from others in his environment. Matthew's vocal behaviors severely affected his ability to participate in activities and had negative social consequences. Many of Matthew's classmates were avoiding him because of his screeching. They often complained if they were seated next to him at circle time, and some children covered their ears when they were near him.

Matthew's team decided to try an intervention to interrupt the behavior and immediately replace it with something functional. The plan was that whenever Matthew screeched or screamed, they would place their hand on his mouth, saying "no noises." They would then immediately ask him to imitate a number of vocal sounds that he knew well.

Some members of Matthew's team felt this procedure was too punitive and unnatural. They wondered whether it might be better to identify some alternative sources of auditory feedback and then gradually strengthen them as choices to replace the screeching. Other members of the team wanted to use a stimulus control strategy—meaning that they would identify an area where Matthew could screech without being disruptive. They acknowledged that it was hard to do that for this behavior, however, since it was so disruptive and loud. Everyone eventually agreed that these strategies would produce change more slowly than the proposed response interruption strategy. Given the negative social consequences already associated with Matthew's behavior, they decided it was best to begin with the procedure that would produce more rapid change.

Once the team began the intervention, they found that the interruption (placing a hand over Matthew's mouth) stopped him from screeching about 50 percent of the time, and the combination of interruption and redirection (asking him to imitate sounds) was successful 90 percent of the time.

After Matthew was screeching less than 10 percent as much as he had at the start of intervention (baseline), his team eliminated the redirection component of the plan. Matthew's vocalizations remained at the same low level with response interruption alone. They then successfully faded the interruption to a simple verbal reminder ("Remember: have a quiet mouth").

Data Collection

As discussed in previous chapters, ABA programs rely on data collection to determine whether an intervention is effective and to make decisions about the need to alter treatment methods. You and your child's team will therefore need to collect data on your child's perseverative vocalizations and how they change in response to intervention. However, collecting data on stereotypic movements and vocalizations is notoriously difficult.

Stereotypic behaviors often occur at a very high rate. These behaviors can be difficult to track because of their frequency; it can seem like they are happening all the time. In the classroom, it is difficult for teachers to track each instance of behavior when they must also attend to other students. At home, parents have other responsibilities and children to take care of. Furthermore, it can be difficult to know when one instance of a vocalization ends and a new one begins. These problems with defining the beginning and end of each behavior make it very hard to track such behaviors using frequency counts—the most common method for tracking behavior.

Methods for Collecting Data on Perseverative Behaviors

Because it is difficult to keep track of how often perseverative behaviors occur, teachers and parents are sometimes asked to collect data on these behaviors during sample times of the day (vs. all day) and/or to use interval recording methods. Common methods of data collection for these kinds of behaviors include momentary time sampling (MTS) and partial interval recording (PI).

Momentary Time Sampling (MTS)

How it works: A timer is set for a specified interval such as 1 minute. When the timer goes off, the teacher or parent looks at the child and records whether or not he is engaging in the behavior at that precise instant.

Question adult asks at the end of the interval: Is the child engaging in the behavior right now (the instant the timer goes off)?

What is recorded? The adult marks a + if the behavior is occurring at that moment and a – if it is not.

What gets calculated? Percent of intervals in which the individual is engaging in the behavior. For example, if the child is vocalizing on 8 out of 10 times that his behavior is sampled, the percentage would be 80%.

Advantages of this approach: MTS is generally extremely easy for teachers or parents to use because it does not require continuous monitoring of the child. The adult simply has to look at the child at that second and indicate what is happening. It does not require the adult to count on a continual basis or to observe in an ongoing or continuous way.

Table 7-1 | Time Sampling Data Sheet

Vocal Stereotypy: repetetive, nonfunctional sounds including loud humming, scripting from songs and commercials, and phrases repeated over and over again. Must be unrelated to context.

1 minute momentary time sample: Behavior recorded if humming or scripting occurring at the moment timer goes off. Behavior during rest of interval not recorded.

Minute	Vocal?	Minute	Vocal?	Minute	Vocal?
:01		:21		:41	
:02		:22		:42	
:03		:23		:43	
:04		:24		:44	
:05		:25		:45	
:06		:26		:46	
:07		:27		:47	
:08		:28		:48	
:09		:29		:49	
:10		:30		:50	
:11		:31		:51	
:12		:32		:52	
:13		:33		:53	
:14		:34		:54	
:15		:35		:55	
:16		:36		:56	
:17		:37		:57	
:18		:38		:58	
:19		:39		:59	
:20		:40		:60	

Partial Interval Recording (PI)

How it works: A timer is set for a specified interval (e.g., 5 minutes). When the timer goes off, the teacher or parent records whether the child has engaged in the behavior *at all* during the interval.

Question adult asks at the end of interval: Did the student engage in the behavior at all during this interval?

What is recorded? A + is recorded if there were any instances of the vocalization in the interval and a – is recorded if there were no instances. The number of times the child engages in the behavior is irrelevant. If the child makes one vocalization during an interval or vocalizes continuously during that interval, that is still recorded as one +.

Table 7-2 | Partial Interval Recording Data Sheet

		DAILY BEHAVIOR DATA COLLECTION			
Name:					
Date:					
Time	Stereotypy	Time	Stereotypy		
9:00-9:05 AM		12:00-12:05 PM		**Operational Definitions**	
9:05-9:10 AM		12:05-12:10 PM		**Vocal Stereotypy:** Defined as any repetitive,	
9:10-9:15 AM		12:10-12:15 PM		nongoal directed or noncommunicative	
9:15-9:20 AM		12:15-12:20 PM		vocalization including humming, repetetive	
9:20-9:25 AM		12:20-12:25 PM		noises, and low level whispered sounds.	
9:25-9:30 AM		12:25-12:30 PM		Must last 3 seconds to be counted	
9:30-9:35 AM		12:30-12:35 PM			
9:35-9:40 AM		12:35-12:40 PM			
9:40-9:45 AM		12:40-12:45 PM			
9:45-9:50 AM		12:45-12:50 PM			
9:50-9:55 AM		12:50-12:55 PM			
9:55-10:00 AM		12:55-1:00 PM		Number of Intervals	
10:00-10:05 AM		1:00-1:05 PM		with stereotypy:	________
10:05-10:10 AM		1:05-1:10 PM			
10:10-10:15 AM		1:10-1:15 PM			
10:15-10:20 AM		1:15-1:20 PM		Total intervals	
10:20-10:25 AM		1:20-1:25 PM		observed	________
10:25-10:30 AM		1:25-1:30 PM			
10:30-10:35 AM		1:30-1:35 PM			
10:35-10:40 AM		1:35-1:40 PM		Percent of	
10:40-10:45 AM		1:40-1:45 PM		intervals:	________
10:45-10:50 AM		1:45-1:50 PM			
10:50-10:55 AM		1:50-1:55 PM			
10:55-11:00 AM		1:55-2:00 PM		Comments:	
11:00-11:05 AM		2:00-2:05 PM			
11:05-11:10 AM		2:05-2:10 PM			
11:10-11:15 AM		2:10-2:15 PM			
11:15-11:20 AM		2:15-2:20 PM			
11:20-11:25 AM		2:20-2:25 PM			
11:25-11:30 AM		2:25-2:30 PM			
11:30-11:35 AM		2:30-2:35 PM			
11:35-11:40 AM		2:35-2:40 PM			
11:40-11:45 AM		2:40-2:45 PM			
11:45-11:50 AM		2:45-2:50 PM			
11:50-11:55 AM		2:50-2:55 PM			
11:55-12:00 PM		2:55-3:00 PM			
TOTAL		TOTAL			

What gets calculated? The percent of intervals in which there were occurrences of the target behavior is calculated.

Advantages of this approach: Partial interval recording does not require complete attention to the child's behavior. The adult does not need to know how much the behavior occurred, only whether it happened at all. Therefore, the adult can still be attending to other children and other tasks, and simply monitoring the child for the occurrence of the behavior. PI does require a higher level of continuous attention to the child, however, than MTS, as the teacher is reporting on the child's behavior throughout the interval (as opposed to only at the end of the interval).

Choosing the Right Data Collection Method

It is important that the data collection method match the characteristics of the behavior. As discussed above, using frequency counts is not likely to be the best way to track instances of stereotyped behavior. Perhaps the most important factor to consider when choosing a way to collect data is whether the parent or teacher can do it in that environment. Is it possible for the parent or teacher to reliably collect data in the planned way? Field testing the data collection system is a good idea. In other words, the parent or teacher should try it once and let the team know what difficulties, if any, they encountered. Finally, data that are collected must be examined on a daily basis so that adjustments in the plan can be made in a timely way.

If the child's vocalizations are not decreasing, the plan is not adequately addressing the problem. In that case, the team should first assess whether the plan is being carried out as planned. If the implementation is fine but the effect is minimal, a new intervention must be considered.

Summary

Perseverative vocalizations are common among children diagnosed with autism spectrum disorders. These behaviors often interfere with learning and with participating in instruction. In addition, peers may be reluctant to interact with children who engage in vocalizations, and these behaviors can lead to stigmatization. Even tolerant and loving family members can find repetitive humming, screeching, or other vocalizations distracting, if not downright annoying. Finally, these types of vocalizations rarely improve without intervention.

The decision as to whether to intervene depends largely on the extent to which the behavior occurs, the degree to which it impairs learning and attention, and the extent to which it is socially undesirable. It may not be necessary to completely eliminate the behaviors. In some cases, intervention is considered successful if the behavior is brought to near zero levels and/or is shaped into a behavior that is more subtle and acceptable.

A variety of behavioral interventions have been shown to be effective in treating perseverative vocalizations in children with autism. A common intervention is environmental enrichment, in which the child is provided with alternative items or sources of reinforcement in hopes that he will eventually prefer using these items to making vocalizations. This strategy may be more likely to succeed if the alternative items provide similar sensory feedback to the vocalizations. A comprehensive and effective treatment package, however, may include additional treatments such as reinforcing the child for using the alternative items appropriately, differential reinforcement procedures, sensory extinction, and response blocking/interruption to effectively reduce the behavior.

Many aspects of the behavior and environment must be considered when deciding upon an intervention, including how often the behavior occurs, how much the behavior interferes with learning, the extent to which the behavior is socially stigmatizing, and how quickly it needs to be reduced. It is possible to make a significant impact on vocal stereotypy with careful assessment and individualized intervention. Assessment must involve determining what function the behavior serves for the child. In the case of vocal stereotypy, it is especially important to evaluate whether it is serving any functions aside from automatic reinforcement.

Some logistical challenges related to treating perseverative behaviors include data collection and deciding whether the behavior warrants intervention. It is important to select a data collection system that can be managed in the home or in the classroom.

As illustrated in the case of John, above, the child can sometimes learn strategies to manage or control the behavior himself. Using these strategies, the child monitors the behavior himself, and requests or initiates the replacement behavior or asks to do it in a permissible location.

As children mature, helping them acquire self-management skills is especially exciting, as these skills involve the child as the agent of his own behavioral change, reducing his dependence on adults for monitoring.

References

Ahearn, W. H., Clark, K. M., MacDonald, R. P. F. & Chung, B. I. (2007). Assessing and treating vocal stereotypy in children with autism. *Journal of Applied Behavior Analysis 40,* 263-75.

Athens, E. S., Vollmer, T. R, Sloman, K. N., & Pipkin, C. S. (2008). An analysis of vocal stereotypy and therapist fading. *Journal of Applied Behavior Analysis 41(2)*, 291-97.

Britton, L. N., Carr, J. E., Landaburu, H. J. & Romick, K. S. (2002). The efficacy of noncontingent reinforcement as treatment for automatically reinforced stereotypy. *Behavioral Interventions 17,* 93–103.

Delmolino, L. & Harris, S. (2004). *Incentives for Change: Motivating People with Autism Spectrum Disorders to Learn and Gain Independence.* Bethesda, MD: Woodbine House.

Dunlap, G., Dyer, K., & Koegel, R. L. (1983). Autistic self-stimulation and intertrial interval duration. *American Journal of Mental Deficiency 88(2),* 194-202.

Favell, J. E., McGimsey, J. F. & Shell, R. M. (1982). Treatment of self-injury by providing alternate sensory activities. *Analysis and Intervention in Developmental Disabilities 2,* 83–104.

Hagopian, L. P. & Toole, L. M. (2009). Effects of response blocking and competing stimuli on stereotypic behavior. *Behavioral Interventions 24,* 117-25.

Hall, S., Thorns, T. & Oliver, C. (2003). Structural and environmental characteristics of stereotyped behaviors. *American Journal of Mental Retardation 108(6),* 391-402.

Higbee T. S, Chang S. & Endicott K. (2005). Noncontingent access to preferred sensory stimuli as a treatment for automatically reinforced behavior. *Behavioral Interventions 20,* 177–84.

Horner, R. H., Carr, E. G., Strain, P. S., Todd A. W. & Reed, H. K. (2002). Problem behavior interventions for young children with autism: A research synthesis. *Journal of Autism and Developmental Disorders* 32(5), 423-46.

Jones, R. S. P. (1999). A 10 year follow-up of stereotypic behavior with eight participants. *Behavioral Interventions 14(1),* 45–54.

Jones, R. S. P., Wint, D., Ellis, N. C. (1990). The social effects of stereotyped behaviour. *Journal of Intellectual Disability Research, 34(3),* 261 – 268.

Kennedy, C. H., Meyer, K. A., Knowles, T. & Shukla, S. (2000). Analyzing the multiple functions of stereotypical behavior for students with autism: Implications for assessment and treatment. *Journal of Applied Behavior Analysis 33(4),* 559–71.

Koegel, R. L. & Covert, A. (1972). The relationship of self-stimulation to learning in autistic children. *Journal of Applied Behavior Analysis 5(4),* 381–87.

Laraway, S., Snycerski, S., Michael, J., & Poling, A. (2003). Motivating operations and terms to describe them: Some further refinements. *Journal of Applied Behavior Analysis 36,* 407-14.

Lovaas, I., Newsom, C., & Hickman, C. (1987). Self-stimulatory behavior and perceptual reinforcement. *Journal of Applied Behavior Analysis 20(1),* 45–68.

Michael, J. (1993). Establishing operations. *The Behavior Analyst 16,* 191–206.

Miller, B. Y. & Jones, R. S. (1997). Reducing stereotyped behaviour: A comparison of two methods of programming differential reinforcement. *British Journal of Clinical Psychology 36*, 297–302

Morrison, K. & Rosales-Ruiz, J. (1997). The effect of object preferences on task performance and stereotypy in a child with autism. *Research in Developmental Disabilities 18(2),* 127-37.

Mueller, M. M. & Kafka, C. (2006). Assessment and treatment of object mouthing in a public school classroom. *Behavioral Interventions 21,* 137-54.

Nijhof, G., Joha, D., & Pekelharing, H. (1998). Aspects of stereotypic behaviour among autistic persons: A study of the literature. *British Journal of Developmental Disabilities 44,* 3-13.

Oliver, C. (1995). Self-injurious behaviour in children with learning disabilities: Recent advances in assessment and intervention. *Journal of Child Psychology and Psychiatry 36(6),* 909–27.

Piazza, C. C., Adelinis, J. D., Hanley, G. P., Goh, H., & Delia, M. D. (2000). An evaluation of the effects of matched stimuli on behaviors maintained by automatic reinforcement. *Journal of Applied Behavior Analysis 33(1),* 13-27.

Rapp, J. T., Dozier, C. L., Carr, J. E., Patel, M. R. & Enloe, K. A. (2000). Functional analysis of hair manipulation: A replication and extension. *Behavioral Interventions 15,* 121–33.

Rapp, J. T., Miltenberger, R. G., Galensky, T. L., Ellingson, S. A. & Long, E. S. (1999). A functional analysis of hair pulling. *Journal of Applied Behavior Analysis 32,* 329–37.

Rapp, J. T., Miltenberger, R. G., Galensky, T. L., Ellingson, S. A., Long, E. S., Stricker, J. & Garlinghouse, M.(2000). Treatment of hair pulling maintained by digital-tactile stimulation. *Behavior Therapy 31*, 381–93.

Repp, A. C., Karsh, K. G., Deitz, D. E. D. & Singh, N. N. (1992). A study of the homeostatic level of stereotypy and other motor movements of persons with mental handicaps. *Journal of Intellectual Disability Research 36(1)*, 61– 75.

Rincover, A. (1978). Sensory extinction: A procedure for eliminating self-stimulatory behavior in developmentally disabled children. *Journal of Abnormal Child Psychology 6*, 299–310.

Ringdahl, J. E., Vollmer, T. R., Marcus, B. A. & Roane, H. S. (1997). An analogue evaluation of environmental enrichment: The role of stimulus preference. *Journal of Applied Behavior Analysis 30,* 203-216.

Roberts-Gwinn, M. M., Luiten, L., Derby, K. M., Johnson, T. A. & Weber, K. (2001). Identification of competing reinforcers for behavior maintained by automatic reinforcement. *Journal of Positive Behavior Interventions 3(2)*, 83-87.

Shabani, D., Wilder, D. & Flood, W. (2001). Reducing stereotypic behavior through self-monitoring and differential reinforcement of other behavior. *Behavioral Interventions 16*, 279-86.

Sidener, T. M., Carr, J. E. & Firth, A. M. (2005). Superimposition and withholding of edible consequences as treatment for automatically reinforced stereotypy. *Journal of Applied Behavior Analysis 38(1),* 121-124.

Singh, N. N., Dawson, M. J. & Manning, P. (1981). Effects of spaced responding DRL on the stereotyped behavior of profoundly retarded persons. *Journal of Applied Behavior Analysis 14,* 521–26.

Tang, J., Patterson, T. G. & Kennedy, C. H. (2003). Identifying specific sensory modalities maintaining the stereotypy of students with multiple profound disabilities. *Research in Developmental Disabilities 25*, 433-51.

Taylor, B. A, Hoch, H. & Weissman, M. (2005). The analysis and treatment of vocal stereotypy in a child with autism. *Behavioral Interventions 20(4)*, 239-53.

Vollmer, T. R. (1994). The concept of automatic reinforcement: Implications for behavioral research in developmental disabilities. *Research in Developmental Disabilities 15(3),* 187-207

Vollmer, T. R., Marcus, B. A. & LeBlanc, L. (1994).Treatment of self-injury and hand mouthing following inconclusive functional analysis. *Journal of Applied Behavior Analysis 27,* 331-44.

8 Repetitive Speech and Echolalia

The previous chapter discusses one type of vocal perseveration that is common in young children with autism spectrum disorders—the repetition of nonspeech sounds. Children with ASD also sometimes perseverate or get stuck on certain words, phrases, or topics of conversation. Although we certainly don't want to discourage children with autism from using speech to communicate, these types of repetitive speech can be just as problematic as the nonspeech perseveration discussed in Chapter 7.

In general, perseverative speech interferes with both social interaction and academic engagement. Children who perseverate with their speech are not open to instruction, as they are often entertaining themselves instead of paying attention to the teacher. It can also be very difficult to help these children develop meaningful social interactions, since others often become frustrated with their repetitive behaviors and narrow ranges of interest.

What Is Perseverative Speech Like?

Below are examples of different types of perseverative speech that children with autism spectrum disorders may engage in. Jessie, Leroy, and Alicia, the children profiled, all have perseverative speech. In many ways, they are like the children we discussed in the last chapter. These behaviors are intrinsically interesting and reinforcing to them, just as the noises and screeches were for children in Chapter 7. Just as for the children with perseverative nonspeech sounds, these children's learning is negatively affected by their perseveration. It is difficult for their parents and teachers to redirect their behaviors, and they often have difficulty following instructions when they are engaging in these behaviors.

Alicia: Using Self-Talk to Entertain Herself

Alicia is a four-year-old with autism. At preschool, she is able to keep up with the group in pre-academic tasks, in group activities, and in play situations. However, she engages in a great deal of perseverative speech that interferes with both her participation and her socialization.

Alicia's favorite movies are Disney Princess movies. She often recites lines verbatim from *Sleeping Beauty, The Little Mermaid,* and *Beauty and the Beast.* (This is sometimes referred to as ***scripting.***) Often, she does this during play, and sometimes it is relevant to the play activity. For example, she may build a castle with blocks and then play with figures saying, "I told you never to go to the West Wing." Often, however, her speech is not related to what is going on. She may simply keep up a running dialog of a scene while the teacher is talking. She may answer someone's question with a line or information from a movie. For instance, recently a child asked for her name, and she said, "Rose, Briarwood Rose."

In addition to using scripting while playing or responding to others, Alicia is sometimes simply in her own world as she plays the scripts in her head. At times she is unresponsive to others in play situations because she is silently running through a script.

Leroy: Talking Obsessively about His Special Interest

Leroy's favorite thing to talk about is monorails. He knows everything about monorails—where they are, how and when they were built, how fast they go, and whether they are operated automatically or by people. When people ask him what he wants to be when he grows up, he says he wants to be a monorail.

Whenever Leroy sees anyone he knows, he wants to talk with them about monorails. He wants to show them his monorail magazines. He wants to show them the stories he has written about Manny the Monorail. Whenever Leroy meets someone new, he tries to find out what they know about monorails. (Have they ever ridden on one? Do they know how monorails are made?)

Leroy even steers conversations into the realm of monorails. Someone may ask him about Halloween, and he will talk about being a monorail for his costume. Someone may mention liking ice cream, and he may say vanilla ice cream is white, like most monorails. It is very disheartening to his parents, as they see others become quickly bored, frustrated, or confused when they interact with Leroy.

Jessie: Using a Favorite Word Excessively

Jessie is a three-year-old girl who loves to say the word "banana." She says it over and over again, and she often answers questions from teachers with the answer followed by "banana." For example, when asked what color a block is, she replies, "blue banana." When asked to state her name, she replies, "Jessie banana." The team is confused about whether they should reinforce her responses when they contain "banana." And they also cannot figure out how to get Jessie to say the correct answer without an added "banana" at the end.

When Jessie first started repeating "banana," it seemed kind of cute. But now it seems distinctly odd.

Interventions for Perseverative Speech

For many children on the autism spectrum, perseverative speech is an automatically reinforced behavior. Children engage in this behavior because they enjoy thinking and talking about a particular topic. In addition, they may lack other skills for interacting, and may fall back on their preferred topics when faced with social interaction.

Given that children often engage in the behavior because they enjoy it or because they don't have the skills to converse with others more appropriately, the two major ways to address perseverative speech are: 1) to make other activities seem more rewarding, and 2) to help the child acquire more advanced language skills. Children can also be redirected, using the response interruption procedure discussed in the previous chapter.

Differential Reinforcement Procedures

The same reinforcement procedures discussed in Chapter 7 that are used to help reduce perseverative nonspeech behaviors can also be used to reduce perseverative speech. Those strategies are:

1. Children can be reinforced for not perseverating (***differential reinforcement of other behavior—DRO***). In this case,

the child is rewarded for the *absence* of the target behavior. As long as they do not engage in perseverative speech, they are rewarded. So, if your child goes 5 minutes without the perseverative speech, she may get a token. After she has earned 5 tokens, she may get computer time.

2. Children can be reinforced for perseverating less than usual (***differential reinforcement of low-rate behavior—DRL***). If a child usually uses perseverative speech approximately every 10 minutes, she may be rewarded if she perseverates 5 or fewer times in a 40-minute period. After successfully meeting those criteria, she may be rewarded for 4 or fewer, 3 or fewer, etc. In this way, the rate is slowly reduced.
3. Children can be reinforced for alternative, appropriate speech (***differential reinforcement of alternative behavior—DRA***). For example, a child who makes requests with odd intonation that makes it difficult to hear might be taught to make her requests with PECS. This increases the effectiveness of her communication and provides her with more reinforcement.

Differential reinforcement procedures can be powerful tools for shaping communication. DRO procedures are easy to implement, and require minimal attention except to determine whether or not the behavior occurred. DRI and DRA procedures build specific behaviors to replace the target behavior. The advantage of these procedures is that they actively build replacement skills. A DRL procedure is useful for building skills that need not be reduced to zero levels.

When using any of these DR procedures, it is important not to purposefully or inadvertently reinforce the behavior you are trying to decrease. Teachers and parents must therefore train themselves not to provide attention for perseverative speech while they are using a DR procedure.

The decision as to which differential reinforcement procedure to use is based on the behavior and on the resources available within the setting.

Jessie: Breaking a Pattern

The intervention for Jessie combined differential reinforcement of other behavior with redirection and response interruption, as described on the next page:

As described above, Jessie frequently followed all her spoken responses with the word banana. It is probable that early on, others inadvertently reinforced this response by laughing or otherwise giving Jessie positive attention when she said banana. The team and her parents knew this, but that did not make the problem easier to address.

They realized that they had to teach Jessie that she would be rewarded only for responses that were appropriate and that did not contain banana. Whenever they could, they reinforced Jessie for responses that did not contain banana. Often, this meant jumping in with reinforcement before she had a chance to say more.

Jessie's team used a variation of response interruption and redirection as well—they provided her with a physical cue on her lips to be quiet after she had said the appropriate part of the response and then they redirected her to do some simple nonvocal imitation tasks. They chose not to do vocal tasks, as those may have been more difficult to redirect.

Finally, the team decided that when Jessie was playing alone in her room, they would not correct her if they heard her using the word banana in her speech. They reasoned that if Jessie learned that it was not acceptable to use the word in public or in a conversation with another person, that would at least limit the behavior's interference in her social interactions.

Teaching New Skills

As mentioned above, one reason that children with autism spectrum disorders engage in perseverative speech may be because they don't have the skills to participate in broader and more diverse conversations. It may be predictable and comforting to them to stick to their best-known topics. They may even wish to interact, but lack the essential skills to make conversation happen. Many children are therefore helped by instruction in conversational skills such as:

1. identifying reciprocal and perseverative conversation;
2. self-monitoring their behaviors;
3. using alternate ways of conversing;
4. learning scripted conversations for practicing these skills.

Increasing Awareness of Appropriate Conversation

Sometimes when a child perseverates on a topic, it may be possible to teach her new social skills that will help reduce the behavior.

Specifically, the child may be helped to understand the inappropriateness of off-task talk through some of the strategies discussed in Chapter 6, such as role-plays or video segments. For example, she might watch a video of someone talking excessively about her special interest while her conversation partners walk away or show by their expressions that they're not interested. She may learn to label examples of perseverative speech as inappropriate and examples of reciprocal conversation as appropriate. Or, even if she is not able to label the behavior, she may learn to recognize that it is not appropriate to do in public, as Alicia did in the case story presented below.

Over time, children with ASD may be able to identify their own appropriate or inappropriate behaviors, and label perseverative speech vs. true reciprocity in conversation. Video self-modeling, as discussed in Chapter 6, may be a useful strategy in teaching this awareness.

Of course, we would not teach young children to use the words perseverative or reciprocal. Instead, we might teach them to say that speech "sounds right" or "can be understood" vs. "sounds wrong" or "can't be understood."

Alicia: "The Talking Place"

Alicia's team wanted to determine how to address her constant repetition of lines from Disney movies, described at the beginning of the chapter. She was not easily redirected, and sometimes she truly resisted attempts to get her to alter the script or stop scripting. Furthermore, her movie-talk seemed to be getting worse over time. While her answers used to make sense about 70 percent of the time, she was now answering in context only about 30 percent of the time. The behavior analyst working with Alicia's team determined that the function of the behavior was automatic reinforcement. In other words, Alicia liked scripts better than any other kind of play or conversation.

The team decided that trying to completely eliminate the behavior was, for now, a bit unrealistic and would likely result in behavioral escalations. Instead, they decided to address Alicia's perseverative speech by helping her differentiate between the situations in which it may be acceptable to repeat lines from movies and the situations in which it is not acceptable. Behavior analysts call this a ***stimulus control procedure.***

To get started, Alicia's team designated a "talking place" in the classroom where Alicia could be redirected whenever she talked about princesses. Whenever she engaged in the behavior, staff would bring her to the area and say, "Oh, you want to talk about movies. You can do that here." The team agreed that they really did not want the procedure to be punitive. Therefore, Alicia was not told this harshly, and it was not implemented as a traditional time-out procedure. The teachers used neutral voices in redirecting Alicia and made sure that the "talking place" was pleasant and comfortable. The staff member set a timer for one minute and then walked away. When the minute was up, the staff member would ask Alicia if she was ready to come back to the group. If she was ready, she could return. If she preferred, she could have an additional minute in the "talking place."

Alicia's teachers initially had some concerns with this procedure. They feared that she could spend her whole day in the talking place. They were reluctant to allow the movie-talk at all, and it seemed counter-intuitive to permit it. Yet everyone acknowledged that redirecting her behavior was completely ineffective, and that data showed her behavior was worsening. Before intervention, the teacher's data indicated that Alicia was engaging in scripting in 60 percent of 5-minute intervals, and that the average duration of scripting was one and a half minutes.

Once the intervention was begun, Alicia's scripting rapidly decreased. The teachers suspended the intervention at one point (called a reversal), to determine if it was in fact the talking place intervention that was responsible for behavior change. When they re-implemented

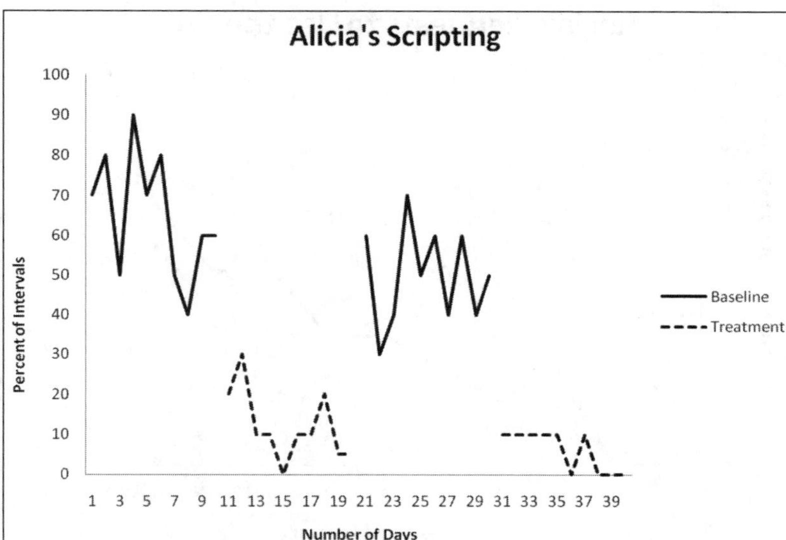

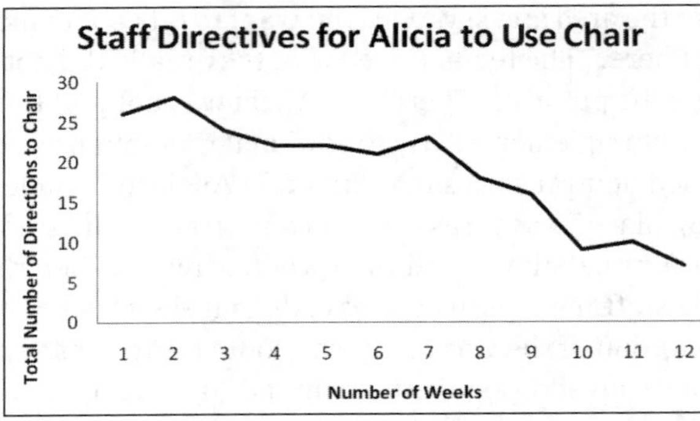

the procedure, they again got the desired behavioral change. The first graph on the previous page shows the effectiveness of the intervention over time and that the procedure was clearly responsible for the improvement in behavior.

Initially, the teachers directed Alicia to the chair many times per day, but over time, they did not have to do this so often. (See graph below of the number of times she was directed to the chair by staff.)

One of the most significant changes was that Alicia did not always need to be explicitly redirected. Over time, she began requesting to go to the talking place (sort of a self-redirection). Sometimes she made

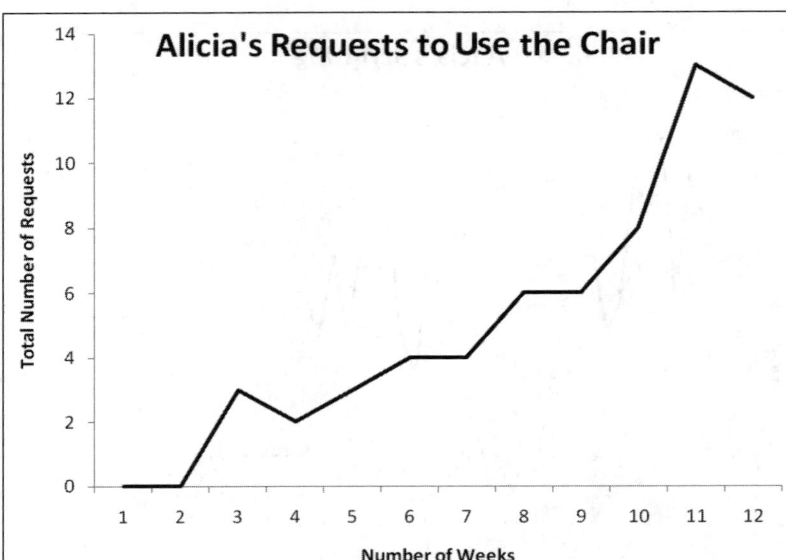

this request even *before* she started repeating lines from movies. This was an exciting development, as it indicated a level of self-control. The increase in her requests for the chair is observable in the last graph.

As Alicia's scripting decreased, everyone was pleased to observe that her appropriate interactions with classmates increased. Data showed that her appropriate responses to peers increased from 34 percent to 78 percent of opportunities.

Overall, allowing Alicia to repeat movie scripts only in a "talking place" was a simple way to teach her that this behavior was only appropriate in a designated place. The team's long-term plans now include requiring Alicia to wait to go to the talking place. In addition, they have discussed eventually giving Alicia only a certain number of requests per day (e.g., cards she can exchange in order to have access to the talking place).

Using Redirection at Home

As a parent, it may be tempting to try using redirection at home, especially if your child's perseverative speech is bothersome and interferes with getting family tasks done. Parents *can* use this procedure at home, but only as part of a comprehensive plan. When you are at home, it can be challenging to constantly attend to behavior and to intervene consistently. It is often easier to extend this procedure to home once it has worked successfully at school.

If you do use redirection at home, it is important to do so systematically and as part of a plan. Be sure to choose a consistent location to redirect your child to. If you use "time-out" with your child, do not use the same location for redirection. When you first start using the procedure, you may want to have some extra help on hand to deal with household demands so that you can focus on redirecting your child with autism in a constant and consistent manner.

Teaching Conversation Skills: Scripts

Besides helping children become more aware of their perseverative speech and the situations when it is appropriate to talk about special interests, the other major way to address repetitive speech is to teach more advanced conversation skills. Chapter 6 offers an overview of the major methods used to teach conversation skills for children with autism, including fill-ins, video modeling, rule cards, and Social Stories.

For children who are verbal but use perseverative speech, we have found that teaching scripted conversation is one of the best ways to improve skills. Scripted conversation can help build conversational skills efficiently and effectively, and can increase the child's confidence in conversing about different topics.

As explained in Chapter 6, ***conversation scripts*** are written or recorded lines that children are taught to use appropriately in given social situations. (This is in contrast to the inappropriate ***scripting*** done by some children who repeat lines from movies and commercials.) Conversation scripts are developed by the child's teachers or parents in response to the child's specific social needs. For example, Isabella, a three-year-old who attends preschool, may have the need to talk with friends about summer vacation. Nick, a five-year-old who is in an after school program, may have the need to talk with friends about sports they participate in. Once a script is written or recorded for a child, the child is taught to use it in context through prompting and reinforcement.

It is important to vary the scripts used. Children with autism need to learn that we do not repeat the identical conversation on multiple occasions. Therefore, it is important to build flexibility into the topic and across topics. Examples of alternate scripts for talking about summer vacation are given below. Each is a five-exchange script. The goal is for the child to be able to converse about a wide range of topics.

Script 1: Summer Vacation
A: Where are you going on summer vacation?
B: We go to a beach house.
A: I love the beach.
B: Me too. We go every year.
A: Cool. What do you do there?
B: We swim in the ocean and play in the sand.
A: Do you build castles?
B: Big castles, with moats and a flag.
A: I like to get buried in the sand.
B: Me too. I get so sandy.

Script 2: Summer Vacation
A: What's your favorite kind of vacation?
B: I love Disney and the beach.
A: I love both of them. The beach is fun.

B: We go to Virginia Beach.
A: Cool. What do you like to do there?
B: We go to the boardwalk and play in the arcade.
A: Are there rides?
B: Yeah, there is a dragon roller coaster.
A: Roller coasters are fun.
B: I can't wait for summer.

Leroy: Expanding the Conversational World

Leroy's main problem was that he was overly focused on monorails. His conversational repertoire was excessively narrow. To be a functional conversational partner, he needed to be able to converse about more topics so others would not be bored or annoyed by his constant talk about monorails.

One of the first things that Leroy's team did was to reinforce him for not engaging in monorail talk. They put him on a DRO procedure (differential reinforcement of other behavior), in which he earned points for every five-minute period that he did not discuss monorails. As he succeeded in this plan, they expanded the timeframes.

At the same time, Leroy's team taught him to engage in conversation about a wide variety of topics. They taught him multiple scripts on ten topics, all of high interest to his peers. For example, they taught him to converse about video games, Thomas engines, Disney movies, and Pokémon cards. They systematically increased the duration of these conversations, beginning with just two back-and-forth exchanges and slowly building to conversations of normal length for his age.

Initially, Leroy's teachers role played the conversations with him. Later, as his skills increased, they involved peers. Peers were primed to ask him certain questions and were taught to reinforce Leroy for appropriate responses. As Leroy's skills expanded, teachers and peers lavishly reinforced him for spontaneous conversation on any of the topics they had taught him, as well as any novel topics.

While the team was helping Leroy increase his conversational repertoire, they also worked on helping him to recognize the elements of appropriate conversation. They showed him videotaped and live examples of perseverative conversation and reciprocal conversation. In some cases, the team acted out conversations. They labeled the good and bad examples for Leroy. They also asked him questions to see if he recognized when a conversation was too repetitive. Over time,

Leroy learned to identify the instances of perseverative speech, and he practiced appropriate reciprocal conversation.

Leroy received reinforcement for all instances of appropriate conversation in practice analog sessions (rehearsed conversations with teachers and parents), in structured play, and in spontaneous situations. Teachers kept daily tallies of instances of good conversations that they observed, and shared their observations with his family. At home, Leroy's sisters started an unplanned incentive program in which they encouraged him to break his record every week, further increasing the social reinforcement available to him for appropriate interaction. When he broke his record, the family had a pizza party, so there was tangible and social reinforcement for his best performance.

What about Echolalia?

When we discuss perseverative or repetitive speech in autism, many people think of echolalia. Echolalia is the repetition of words or phrases, often done immediately after hearing the words or phrases. For example, a teacher may say, "Hi Melinda." And the child replies, "Hi Melinda." Or a classmate may ask, "Do you like Batman?" And the child with autism may reply, "Do you like Batman?" Some children also repeat words after a delay. For instance, they may repeat a sentence their parent said a few days earlier or a line from a movie they watched in the past. This is closer to scripting.

Immediate echolalia is a complex behavior that may tell us more about a child's language development than perseveration does. In other words, echolalia may be a phase of language development for some children. It also may reflect a lack of understanding of the meanings of words and a lack of reciprocity in their interactions with others.

One of the challenges in addressing echolalia is that we do not want to punish attempts at speech when it is just emerging. Any intervention must therefore be approached with some caution, to ensure that we do not inadvertently discourage all vocal communication.

Sometimes, differential reinforcement may be a helpful intervention. That is, when the child speaks without echolalia, she is reinforced much more elaborately than she is for responses with echolalia. For example, you might ask your child her name and she may reply, "What is your name? Amelia." In this case, you might just smile at her. But if she answers, "Amelia," you might tickle her, give her a high five, and tell her how proud you are of her. This procedure can lead to an increase of responses without echolalia and decrease of responses with echolalia.

If a child customarily uses echolalia, it can be a daunting task to get her to stop. Sometimes, however, teachers and parents can use a vocal volume cue to get the child to respond without echolalia. Specifically, you can try saying what you *want* your child to say louder than the other words. For example, you may say, "What is your name [whispering]? Say [whispering] Joey [louder]." If a child can read, you might use a textual prompt. For example, you might present the child a card with the word "Joey" on it when you ask him his name. Textual prompts can often help reduce the echoing of all words.

Managing Perseveration in the Real World

It can be very difficult for family members to tolerate perseverative vocalizations. This is true whether we are referring to noises or to speech. It can be extremely trying if your child is making noises as others are trying to eat, sleep, think, talk on the phone, do homework, or talk. Likewise, if your child is scripting from a movie as the family is trying to converse, it can be very annoying and disruptive. Similarly, a child who wants to talk about her favorite topic all day long can wear away at the tolerance and patience of parents and siblings.

If your child is in an ABA program, you and your family will be given suggestions on how to address the behavior over the long term. In the moment, however, it may not always be possible to react in the best possible way. You may need to ignore your child's behavior in certain circumstances, or, particularly in the car, you may want to provide everyone with a break by playing music over the sound of your child's scripting or noises. While these strategies may not be part of the official plan, they happen as people imperfectly navigate the complexities of family life.

Generally, the recommendations we make about managing these behaviors are individually tailored. As discussed previously, for some children, the reinforcement of engaging in perseverative speech or vocalizations is largely internal. They just enjoy the behavior. If your child is in this position, the goal is to come up with redirection strategies and rules that limit the extent to which perseveration takes over your child's experience.

Sometimes, perseverative behavior may take on other functions. For example, a child may have learned that scripting is very irritating to her family. She may therefore repeat lines from movies to get negative attention from others. That is, being told to "Stop that!" is actually reinforcing to some children, as it provides individualized attention. Another child may use perseverative speech in order to obtain the lollipops that were originally offered to her in order to redirect her from perseverating. If secondary functions such as these are identified for your child's behaviors, you will be advised not to provide these types of maintaining reinforcers to your child, if at all possible.

Perhaps the most important thing for parents to do at home is to collect data. This can help provide objective indications of change in your child's behavior. Perseverative behaviors can be so irritating that it can be very difficult to objectively know whether things are improving. Collecting data can provide hope when they show that these behaviors actually are improving. Data can also help you and your child's team to identify when interventions are not adequately working, which can lead to quicker alterations in strategies.

Summary

The examples above demonstrate how vocal stereotypy can be addressed in many different ways. Intervention might include:

- shaping the perseverative behavior into more acceptable behaviors,
- finding different, less stigmatizing ways for your child to get the same type of stimulation,
- reinforcing your child when she uses the problematic behaviors less frequently, and
- helping her understand contexts in which such behaviors are permissible and not permissible.

Reference

Ahearn, W. H., Clark, K. M., MacDonald, R. P. F. & Chung, B. I. (2007). Assessing and treating vocal stereotypy in children with autism. *Journal of Applied Behavior Analysis 40,* 263-75.

9 Fluency: Making Sure Skills Are Available When They Are Needed

In earlier chapters of this book, we have discussed the importance of being able to make fluent responses. To be functional, a child's skills must not only be mastered, but must be mastered well enough to be used in the contexts and situations where they are needed. Helping children become fluent ensures that skills are useable, available, and able to be drawn on as needed.

Ben

Ben is a four-year-old on the autism spectrum who has learned many skills through ABA instruction, and is now spending part of his instructional time in a preschool classroom. He is generally responsive and engaged in his preschool class, and he can follow directions and attend to a teacher in a group. Sometimes, however, his behavior is off-putting to his peers. For example, he likes to play with toys in only one way, and objects when anyone does something novel or different with them. During transitions, he sometimes screams loudly. And he often has a tantrum when he can't do something he likes to do, such as play with the trains.

Socially, Ben has some interest in others and is generally responsive to his peers. However, he doesn't react quickly to his classmates when they interact with him, and he can take an unusually long time to respond.

His team first noticed Ben's slow reaction time when children began greeting Ben during his initial visits to the classroom. The children were eager to put their new classmate at ease and to welcome him to class. Many of them approached him and either said "hello" or asked him his name. Responding appropriately to greetings and giving his name when asked were skills Ben had mastered many months before joining the preschool class. In fact, he could reliably answer these kinds of questions and responded to such social overtures very consistently.

In the new classroom, Ben's shadow (aide) noticed that although Ben consistently responded, his responses were always delayed. It took him too long to answer his classmates. Often, by the time he answered, his classmates were gone, having moved on to someone or something else.

Ben's shadow decided to objectively evaluate how long it was taking him to respond, so she took data on the latency to respond. Specifically, she timed how many seconds elapsed before Ben actually answered his friends. Her data indicated that it took Ben an average of 7 seconds before he replied. Sometimes it took him 10 seconds. He almost never replied before 5 seconds had elapsed.

Now, 5, 7, and 10 seconds do not sound like long timeframes. But in the world of social conversation, they are VERY LONG indeed. (Try counting out 7 seconds in your mind, and think about how long that would feel if you were waiting for a social response! Now imagine how long that would feel for three- or four-year-old preschoolers. Their attention is fleeting and their patience is limited.) In nearly every case, Ben missed out on the opportunity to socialize. His classmates had moved on, and were not present to hear his response.

Ben's team members were a bit perplexed. How could they not have anticipated this issue? Had they missed this aspect of his responding? Had they failed to notice a salient and really significant quality of his interactions with others? Why had they missed it? How could they not have better prepared Ben for this environment? And most importantly, how could they fix the problem? They wanted to fix the problem quickly, because they feared that Ben's slow responses would discourage the other children from approaching him or including him in activities.

In fact, they were right to be concerned. Peers' greetings and attempts to interact with Ben had already decreased. It was hard to know whether this was because the peers had become used to his presence (i.e., the novelty had worn off) or whether it was a consequence of his poor responses. However, the shadow did overhear some comments from the children indicating that Ben's communication style was a factor. They said things to one another such as, "Don't go—he won't answer you"; "He doesn't like it when you talk to him"; or "He doesn't talk."

Ben's team was especially concerned about those statements and explanations, as they indicated that the peers perceived Ben as avoidant, disinterested, and/or incapable of responding to them. They predicted that if Ben was thought of as disinterested or as preferring to be left alone, his peers would be less likely to try to play or talk with him. In fact, this turned out to be true. (Data showed a large reduction in social bids and greetings by peers.) Ben now got fewer opportunities to interact, and was becoming more isolated in the classroom environment, spending much of his free time alone.

The Concept of Fluency

One way to think about Ben's problems in interacting with his classmates is that Ben was simply not fluent. While he did answer people's questions, he could not do it in a timeframe that was functional. When a child cannot respond fluently, it has serious social consequences, including missed opportunities for social interaction and classroom participation.

Fluency—in reference to any skill—refers to the combination of accuracy plus speed that characterizes competent performance (Binder, 1996). Most of us are fluent in many, many skills. There are numerous examples from each of our own lives. For example, when we leave our homes in the morning and drive to work, we do not need to think through all the steps of moving the car (insert key, turn key, put car in reverse, back out of driveway, put car in drive, hit gas pedal). We have attained a level of automaticity in driving; we no longer have to think through each step of the task. When we were brand new to driving, each of those components required careful attention. As our experience increased, and we logged more and more hours of driving, we no longer had to concentrate on each element of the task. We were able to simply do those actions without forethought, planning, or hesitancy.

Similarly, think of how you make a sandwich to take in your lunch. Often, people make sandwiches during a very hectic time of the morning. They may be thinking about their day, talking to family members, and multitasking while doing many other activities related to preparation for the day. Generally, we are able to continue making sandwiches despite a multitude of interruptions and interfering thoughts. When such interruptions occur, they generally do not lead to errors in sandwich making. We can maintain our focus, work with accuracy, and achieve the goal easily and without much effort. You can think of many more examples from your own life—skills you can do well, quickly, effortlessly, and without thinking.

Achieving fluency is considered important for the functional demonstration and use of any skill. When skills are fluent, they have several important characteristics:

- stability,
- endurance,
- application, and
- retention.

Stability refers to the ability to engage in the behavior in the face of distraction for long periods of time. For example, if you think back to some of the examples given of everyday tasks that are associated with fluency, stability of response is clear. You can make a sandwich in a quiet environment, but you can also make a sandwich in a house full of hustle and bustle, while the phone is ringing, and while conversing with others in the house about the upcoming events of the day. Similarly, you can drive a car with the radio on, while talking on the phone, or while speaking with other passengers. These skills are stable; that is, you can do them despite a myriad of environmental distractions.

Endurance refers to the ability to engage in the skill for a long period of time. I can drive my car for fifteen minutes, but I can also drive my car for three hours. I can make seven sandwiches just as well as I can make one sandwich. My accuracy does not diminish simply as a function of having to do the skill for longer periods.

Application refers to the ability to transfer skills (and sometimes to the ability to combine related skills in novel ways). I can make tuna fish sandwiches and peanut butter and jelly sandwiches and ham sandwiches. I can drive many different kinds of cars with relative ease. A new driver is intimidated by the novel arrangement of dials and con-

trols on the dashboard in an unfamiliar vehicle, while an experienced driver adapts fairly readily. This is an example of application, or transfer of fluent skills.

Retention refers to the maintenance of skills in the absence of practice. I can take a trip to Italy for two weeks and not drive at all while I'm on vacation. But when I land at the airport and find my car in the parking lot, I have no trouble remembering how to turn it on and drive home.

Implications of a Lack of Fluency

Lack of fluency in any skill can be frustrating and discouraging for the individual. As illustrated by the story of Ben, above, lack of fluency in social or language skills can have wide-ranging effects. A child who responds to a peer's invitation to play ten seconds after it is issued may very well miss the chance to play. Similarly, if a student is called on by the teacher in a group and doesn't answer in a timely way, the lesson may move on. Some students are aware that they missed the chance to play or to show the teacher that they knew the answer. They may feel discouraged about their slow response time, about not keeping up with the group, and about being perceived as less able than they are. These feelings can exacerbate the difficulties. Even if children are not aware of their lack of fluency, they will probably lose out on opportunities for socializing and practicing language that they might have had if they responded more fluently.

Difficulties with fluency can be demonstrated in many ways. As already discussed, they can be manifested by a lack of appropriate speed or by delays in responding. When we watch someone do something that he is not fluent at, his actions may seem laborious. It may look like it is difficult for him to complete the task or to concentrate on the task at hand. Think about watching a child learn to ride a bike or use roller skates. It does not look fluid or smooth; it looks effortful. Think about how a young child sounds when learning to read. It is often very difficult for him to sound out each word, and it may take him an inordinately long time to read many words on a page. These examples highlight how slow and difficult nonfluent skills can appear.

Other consequences of a lack of fluency are best understood in the context of time. If we are not fluent in our ability to do a task, it will take us an excessive amount of time to complete a task, compared to fluent performers. Someone who is a fluent reader may read a page in two minutes, while someone who is not fluent may take ten minutes. Accuracy alone is insufficient, especially in academic environments and social contexts. A student who takes twelve seconds to answer a teacher's question at circle time will stand out as unresponsive and may be perceived as unable to answer, even though he has the ability to do so. A lack of fluency has real-life implications.

Focusing on Fluency within ABA Treatment

Without specific intervention, children with autism are often nonfluent in performing many skills. Their responses are often slow and laborious, it takes them longer to do tasks others do rapidly, and they often have excessively long pauses before responding.

In the past, ABA intervention for autism has focused less on speed than on accuracy (e.g., Fabrizio & Moors, 2003). In general, individuals have been considered competent in skills if they can demonstrate them correctly at a specified percentage of times. For example, a student may be considered to have mastered a program if he can demonstrate the skill 90 percent of the time, regardless of how long it takes him to do the skill. Sometimes, these definitions are expanded to include criteria for consistency of skill demonstration (e.g., across 3 days) or transfer/generalization of skills (e.g., across 3 instructors). Sometimes criteria also specify aspects of skill performance that are time-based. For example, we could require that the response begin within a certain number of seconds (e.g., Joey will respond to a friend's greeting within 2 seconds) or be completed within a certain number of seconds (e.g., Joey will do a 3-piece puzzle within 10 seconds).

In recent years, we have been paying more attention to the role of timely responses when defining competent performance for children with autism (e.g., Fabrizio & Moors, 2003; Weiss, 2005). Now a skill is not considered mastered simply because the individual can perform it correctly. To be a functional skill, responses must also be timely. For example, social responses must occur in a certain timeframe to be reinforced by others. When Ben took 5, 7, or 10 seconds to respond to his classmates, it was simply too long. Preschool-aged friends can't wait that long for a response. If a teacher asks a child a question during circle time, she cannot wait 15 seconds for a response. If she did, she would risk losing the attention of the 18 other young students in her care. Responding to others quickly is, in fact, is an essential aspect of skill mastery.

For all of these reasons, speed of response has been receiving more attention in intervention for children with autism. Clinicians have been noticing the social consequences of slow response times. In a variety of ways, we are now evaluating and addressing issues in slow response time. As mentioned above, often speed of performance is simply integrated into the definitions of competent performance and into the criteria for skill mastery. Systematically reducing how long a child is given to reply or to complete a response can be extremely effective in addressing these time-based response issues. As discussed in the next section, some instructors are also using timed practice to build speed of response.

Timed Practice

Timed practice involves helping the child perform a skill as quickly as possible. The child learns to respond at a much faster rate than he would need to demonstrate in the natural environment. This high speed practice builds the automaticity of the child's response. When responses are automatic, they are *available* to the learner. A child can demonstrate the fluent skill without hesitation and without difficulty.

Within ABA, a procedure/strategy known as ***Precision Teaching*** focuses on building fluent responding, either once a skill has been established or from the start of training. In precision teaching approaches, the *rate* at which skills are demonstrated is centrally important. In other words, it is not enough for someone to be able to do something correctly; he or she must also be able to do it *quickly*. Real competence requires both accuracy (getting it right) and speed (doing it quickly).

Within Precision Teaching, rate-building is done in timed practices until the goal speed is achieved. (See the continuation of Ben's story, below, for examples of how timed practices are done.) Goal speeds are determined in a variety of ways. For example, if a young child with ASD needs to increase the speed at which he answers yes and no questions or responds to others' greetings, his teachers might refer to "compiled rates" (e.g., Kubina, Morrison, & Lee, 2002). These are average times for doing various skills that were collected over time and from multiple age ranges and populations.

Another way to choose a goal speed for a child with autism is to refer to the data published by M. Fabrizio and A. Moors (Fabrizio and Moors, 2003). These researchers collected data on the ranges of speed at which individuals with autism demonstrated various skills at a fluent level. In this study, a skill was only considered to be fluent if the individual could demonstrate it with:

- stability (the ability to engage in the task in the presence of distraction),
- endurance (stamina, the ability to do the task for long periods of time),
- application (transfer of skills or generalization), and
- retention (maintenance of skills despite lack of practice).

It is also possible for instructors to choose goal speeds by observing how quickly other children do the given skill. Of course, the sample can be done on peers who are the same age to increase the likelihood of choosing an appropriate target speed.

Ben, Continued

Ben's team first wanted to evaluate where the breakdown occurred in Ben's responsiveness so they could use the information to determine how best to address his delays in responding to others. They decided to systematically evaluate his lag times in responding in all different situations. They collected data on how long it took him to respond to teachers in his familiar home instruction environment, to teachers in the novel school environment, to siblings and neighbors at home, and to his peers in the new classroom environment.

Essentially, Ben's team wanted to tease apart the factors associated with slow responding. Was it a function of the classroom environment? If so, perhaps Ben had trouble with the visual and auditory distractions of the classroom environment. Was it a function of child vs. adult interaction? Maybe Ben was responsive to adults, with whom he had a strong learning history and lots of experience in responding to, and less so to peers, with whom he had less experience. Was it a function of familiarity? Maybe Ben responded more quickly to people he knew well.

What Ben's team discovered was that he had no difficulties with responding in familiar contexts to familiar people. This alleviated some of their concern about having possibly missed his slow response rate before he moved on to preschool.

Ben's team decided to address his slow response rate in the classroom in several ways:

- *They required that he respond within two seconds to every question or greeting. If he did not, they prompted him to do so.*
- *In addition, they decided to give Ben extra practice in these skills, so they began increasing the number of opportunities he had to practice these skills every day. They made sure that some of these practice opportunities happened outside of his work room both at school and at home and with less familiar people in the neighborhood (including some neighborhood children).*
- *Ben's team also started timed practice for greetings. They ran the timed practice in two ways, both of which were presented as games (see the section below).Initially, these games were done with small groups of family members, neighbors, and therapists.*

In these ways, Ben's team tried to help Ben generalize his skills from the previous educational environment to the new classroom. They recognized the need for more practice in less familiar contexts.

Orienting to and greeting others

***Introduction of the game:** The instructor reviewed a rule card which stated that Ben was to look at the person indicated and say hi. She also reviewed the goal of going as quickly as possible. In fact, she shared with Ben exactly how many greetings he needed to get to meet his goal, and showed him that on a number chart.*

***Mechanics of practice:** Ben sat facing the group of children, who were seated in a semicircle in front of him. A second instructor sat behind* *the group. Instructor number one set a timer for the target number of seconds. Then the instructor pointed randomly to one person at a time. Ben had to look at and greet that person. The other child returned Ben's greeting, but the instructor did not wait for that interaction to be completed before moving on to the next person. (This was because Ben was practicing going as fast as he could; timed practice involved doing the skill at unnaturally high speeds, faster than would actually be required in the natural environment.)While the game was going on, the second instructor used a clicker (golf counter) to keep track of how many times Ben said "hi."*

After the sprint: *When the timer went off, the instructor looked at the counter to see the number of responses, and shared this information with the group. If Ben met his goal, the whole group did a hip hip hooray cheer for Ben. (Ben also received an individual reward that was highly preferred.) If Ben did not meet his goal, he could try again then or after some other members of the group had their turns. The same rules were reviewed and each other member of the group participated in the game.*

Reciprocating a greeting

Introduction of the game: *The instructor reviewed a rule card which stated that Ben was to find who was greeting him, look at him or her, and respond to the person using his or her name. She also reviewed the goal of going as quickly as possible. Once again, she shared with Ben exactly how many responses he needed to get to meet his goal in the allotted time, and showed him that on a number chart.*

Mechanics of practice: *Ben sat facing the children, who were seated in a semicircle in front of him. The instructor sat behind Ben. She cued each member of the group with a photo and textual cue card to greet Ben. This was done randomly, not in any predictable order. Ben's task was to find the person greeting him, establish eye contact with him or her, and greet him or her by name (e.g., "Hi, Miranda"). As in the previous game, the pace was unusually fast, much faster than the rate at which interactions in a group naturally occur.*

After the sprint: *When the timer went off, the instructor looked at the counter to see the number of responses, and shared this information with the group. If Ben met his goal, the whole group sang a song of Ben's choice. (Ben also received a chosen individual reward.) If Ben did not meet* *his goal, he might try again immediately or after some other members of the group had their turns. For each additional participant, the same rules were reviewed and the same format was followed.*

Comments on Timed Practice

The examples above show how timed practice can be used to help young children with autism become more fluent with social communication skills. For Ben, staff members created mock situations that mimicked the final goal task and presented them as games. In the first situation, Ben simply responded to other children's greetings. In the second situation, Ben had to locate his communicative partner and respond to him or her. Ben was given many practice opportunities, and individual and group incentives were used to make the activity highly rewarding.

For young children with ASD, a variety of common skills can be targeted with timed practice, including:

- responding to greetings
- initiating greetings
- answering social questions (e.g., What is your name? How are you today?)

While it is exciting to see the progress in fluency a child makes in timed practice sessions, the bottom line in communication and socialization is what happens in the real world. In other words, we need to determine whether the child can transfer his fluent skills into the natural environment.

In Ben's case, staff members tracked his progress in the timed practice, but they also gathered data on his responses in the classroom setting outside of timed practice sessions. They tracked the percentage of opportunities in which Ben answered in an acceptable period of time. These data showed that his timed practice sessions were a successful intervention.

In determining how and whether to use timed practice with a child on the autism spectrum, the key is individualization. Not all children with autism have serious difficulties in responding in a timely way. Some may not need any specific attention to this issue. Others have trouble with fluency only in some situations, such as in groups, in novel environments, or with new material. Targeting those troublesome situations can be very helpful for those children. Some children with autism are globally slow, and may have long gaps in responsiveness in all situations. These children may benefit the most from focused training in responding quickly.

Fluency Problems at Home

Children with autism spectrum disorders often respond nonfluently at home. For example, your child may take a very long time to answer when you ask him what he would like to drink with dinner, or it may seem to take forever for him to answer questions about his school day. Timed practice will eventually address those long lag times in responding.

In the meantime, you can note long gaps in response time, and can prompt your child after a few seconds. In some cases, you can simply repeat the question. In other cases, you might offer a choice (e.g., "milk or apple juice?").

What you do *not* want to do is to assume that your child will never be able to respond in a more timely way. Sometimes, we make assumptions about a child's processing ability that are not entirely accurate. Often, children with autism can learn to respond more quickly with practice, encouragement, and the requirement to do so. It is sometimes tempting for logistical and emotional reasons to simply provide them with items without addressing these lags in responding. (For example, you might go ahead and give your child what you think he wants if he doesn't respond quickly when you ask what he wants to drink.) However, working with your child on his response time can have a much more positive impact for both you and your child.

References

Binder, C. (1996). Behavioral fluency: Evolution of a new paradigm. *The Behavior Analyst 19(2),* 163-97.

Fabrizio, M. & Moors, A. (2003). Evaluating mastery: Measuring instructional outcomes for children with autism. *European Journal of Behavior Analysis 4(1),* 23-36.

Kubina, R. M., Morrison, R., & Lee, D. L. (2002). Benefits of adding precision teaching to behavioral interventions for students with autism. *Behavioral Interventions 17,* 233-46.

Weiss, M. J. (2005). Comprehensive ABA Programs: Integrating and evaluating the implementation of varied instructional approaches. *Behavior Analyst Today 6(4),* 249-56.

10 The Role of Siblings

Typically developing brothers and sisters are constantly communicating with each other at home and in the community. They make comments to one another, ask each other questions, and play games that require verbal interactions. They quarrel, they argue, and they call each other names. As they grow older, they have real conversations and gossip with each other. All of these interactions help them develop their receptive and expressive communication skills and learn how to use language in real-life situations (pragmatics).

When one or more of the siblings has an autism spectrum disorder, normal communicative interactions are disrupted, at least to a certain degree. A major reason for this disruption is that most young children with ASD respond inconsistently to others. Often, they are less responsive to other children than they are to adults. Siblings, therefore, often feel ignored.

The child with autism may also engage in behaviors that make effective communication quite challenging for siblings. They may screech, repeat words or phrases, or respond with sounds or words that do not make sense. Even children with good speech and language skills may want to talk only about a few restricted topics. This can make reciprocal conversation challenging.

A sibling's efforts to interact with her brother or sister with ASD may fail more often than not. If this pattern continues, the sibling may become frustrated and reduce or stop her attempts to interact with her brother or sister. Siblings may simply begin to quietly coexist alongside their brother or sister, rather than trying to be his or her partner in play. Siblings may also experience challenging emotions related

to the communication difficulties of their brother or sister with autism. They may be afraid when their sibling is upset and cannot communicate what is wrong. They may worry that the escalation may become uncontrollable, and they may feel helpless to change the outcome. They may also be irritated, annoyed, or angry when the communication challenges and behavioral outbursts create tension, change family plans, and otherwise influence the course of family life.

When siblings with and without autism experience these kinds of problems communicating with one another, there can be undesirable side effects for everyone involved:

- It may increase the isolation of both children.
- It certainly means the loss of opportunities for social interaction, and for teaching important social skills.
- It also prevents both siblings from experiencing each other in positive ways, which helps to strengthen the sibling bond.
- Finally, parents often feel very sad and disappointed when their children struggle to play together.

Core Skills to Help Siblings Communicate

There are certain skills that can help siblings be more successful in their interactions with their brother or sister with autism. These skills center on making the child with autism more responsive to their sibling. It is also helpful to pair the sibling with positive things, so that the child learns to enjoy being with his or her sibling and chooses to interact with him or her. Important skills to focus on include:

1. getting attention,
2. prompting, and
3. reinforcing.

Getting Attention

Often, children with autism ignore their siblings' social overtures. One strategy to increase the likelihood that your child with autism will respond to a request is to make sure that she is paying attention before the instruction is given.

In some cases, such as when asking a question, it is natural to first get the child's attention (e.g., "Hey Amy..."). In other types of interactions, we often begin speaking before gaining attention. This may lead to missed opportunities and failed responses between siblings. It might be helpful to teach your other children to always make sure they get their brother or sister's attention first. Tell them to make sure their sibling is looking at them before they start talking. Also encourage them to try again if he or she does not respond the first time.

Christopher never did what Michael wanted, so Michael just gave up. When he went over to his brother, his brother didn't even notice. He just kept doing whatever he was doing (usually lining things up and peering at them through a squinted eye). Then one day, Michael's mom showed him what she had learned at Chris's school. They had taught her that Chris would be much more likely to respond to her if she got his attention first. She showed Michael how she did it. She called Christopher's name, and she waited for him to look at her. When he did, she gave him some praise and asked him to do something else (such as giving her a high five, touching his nose, giving her the fire truck). Michael saw that Chris did not ignore his mom. He also saw that his brother could do a lot of things, if he was paying attention.

There are other ways for siblings to get their brother's or sister's attention. For example, they might bring their brother or sister a treat, a favorite toy, or an item that has interesting sounds or textures. They might make a silly noise, or otherwise engage in silly behavior. Many of these interactions are more natural, more playful, and more like what typical siblings do to gain one another's attention. You can encourage siblings to explore different ways to gain attention, but make sure they are always engaging voluntarily in these interactions. Also make sure that your child with autism consents to, and is comfortable with, these interactions.

This training must be done with some caution and sensitivity, especially if your child with autism is older than her sibling(s). It is not appropriate for the typically developing sibling to be ordering her older sibling with autism around. The interactions between children should be fun or at least tolerable for both children, and neither should feel coerced or burdened by having to interact. In addition, many children with autism have difficulty tolerating social interaction, so expecting them to respond to too many demands from their siblings could lead to behavioral escalations. It is also important for the sibling to try to get her brother or sister's attention when she is not otherwise immersed in an activity. Furthermore, she should only ask her brother or sister to do things he or she knows how to do.

Prompting

Siblings can also be taught to help their brother or sister make the right response. For example, you can teach them how to show your child with autism how to do something (such as by modeling the correct response). If your children are playing with the train set, the sibling might ask her brother to put a train on a bridge. As she gives this instruction, she could put a train on the bridge, so that her brother can simply copy her action. She could also point to the bridge to give him a hint about the desired behavior.

One of the problems that Paige had with Owen was that he hardly ever did what she asked him to. Even when she got his attention first, he often just seemed to ignore her. She told her parents that she thought he didn't like her and that she didn't want to keep trying to get him to do things.

The behavior analyst working with the family thought that Paige would feel differently if she could rely on Owen responding. She taught Paige to make sure that Owen did what she said by helping him get the answers right. She called it the "no failing class," and Paige thought that was funny. When they did toy play, Paige modeled actions for Owen to imitate. When they reviewed picture cards, she pointed to the right one. When she asked him a question, she answered first, and then he imitated her. Page started assigning imaginary grades to Owen in her "no failing class." While the grades didn't have meaning for Owen, they helped Paige gauge how her brother was doing. They also reminded her to help him, and they reinforced her efforts to prompt correct responses.

It is much more difficult to prompt nonmotor responses. Any speech responses are harder to prompt. However, your children can learn to prompt their brother or sister to answer vocally by providing the initial sound of a word. For example, to prompt the response "juice," they can say "What do you want? Ju—."

In general, it is easier to initially teach siblings to help their brother or sister with nonvocal tasks. Over time, as siblings get more accustomed to helping their brother or sister, the tasks might be expanded.

Reinforcing

Perhaps most importantly, siblings can be taught to reward their brother or sister for listening to them, playing with them, and responding to requests. They can be taught how to provide praise, which can be done in ways that are socially appropriate for kids (e.g., high fives). They can also be taught to provide more tangible rewards such as a Koosh ball, silly band, or favorite toy. Older children might even give their sibling with autism tokens if he or she receives tokens for appropriate responses.

Ethan was very unresponsive to his sister Josie. He learned to listen to her, but he was not interested in her rewards. In fact, he would go to his mother for rewards whenever he was working or playing with his sister. His sister liked that Ethan had learned to respond to her, but wanted him to come to her for rewards too. Her mom suggested that she sing Ethan's favorite songs to him as soon as he did something she asked. Ethan started staying near her to hear the songs. Sometimes when she paused, Ethan would even fill in the missing words. As time went on, Josie also began making silly faces, speaking in goofy voices, and otherwise socially entertaining him.

In the beginning, when siblings are helping their brother or sister learn a new skill such as listening to them or responding to them, they should provide reinforcement frequently—just as when parents or teachers are teaching a new skill. At first, siblings should reinforce every correct response. It may even be a good idea for them to reinforce their brother or sister just for tolerating them as teachers. As your child with autism makes progress and adjusts to the demands, her siblings will need to reduce the rewards and provide more typical positive feedback and reactions. Eventually, an enthusiastic response from her siblings should be enough of a reward for your child with autism.

You will probably need to help your children learn not to inadvertently reinforce inappropriate behaviors. For example, siblings may naturally react to behaviors they find annoying (e.g., whining) or distasteful (e.g., spitting). They may be inclined to give their brother or sister snacks to quiet whining, or to yell at their brother or sister for spitting. In some cases, these reactions might lead to *more* whining or spitting. You will therefore need to let siblings know when to ignore behaviors so as not to increase their rate.

In talking with your children about their interactions with their brother or sister with autism, it is wise to let them know that situations will often crop up that require some thinking. Let them know that you and their brother's or sister's teachers may need to come up with plans to deal with new behaviors to help make sure these behaviors do not become real problems.

Involving Siblings in Treatment Sessions

Sometimes parents decide to have siblings join some treatment sessions. This can have multiple advantages. It certainly makes it possible to focus on social skills in sessions, and can give the child with autism opportunities to build skills such as sharing teacher attention and following group instructions. It can also demystify the treatment for your other children. Often, siblings enjoy seeing what actually happens in the sessions. It can help siblings understand that their brother or sister is working hard in the sessions, not simply playing. This can reduce any jealousy associated with the increased attention their brother or sister is receiving. In addition, when siblings are included in treatment sessions, they can work on learning to get their brother or sister's attention, prompting strategies, and providing reinforcement.

Supporting the Needs of All the Children in the Family

Although we have suggested various ways that siblings can help the child with autism increase her communication skills, that is not to imply that brothers and sisters should be regarded as miniature parents or teachers. As in all families, the goal for parents is to foster the most normal, harmonious relationships between siblings. It goes without saying that parents need to be careful to support the developmental needs of *all* their children.

One important way to help other children in the family with their own support needs is to arrange for them to meet other siblings of children with autism. Many siblings enjoy learning that there are other kids who live in families with people with autism. Sibling groups, sibling visiting days, and sibling pen pal programs can all be used to build links between siblings of children with autism. As any parent with a child with autism knows, there is a special kind of support to be found in others who share your circumstance. Another child who lives with similar challenges can provide your children with a type of support that is entirely unique and unavailable elsewhere.

Families should also feel free to ask the members of their child's team for assistance in supporting the sibling's needs. Clinicians can help them to explain autism in developmentally appropriate ways, encourage open expression of feelings, and become a resource to families about sibling needs.

Your family should also feel free to ask team members for guidance in treating your children equally, or at least help in explaining inequitable treatment. This is important because a recent study suggested that parental inequities may harm the relationship between siblings (Rivers & Stoneman, 2008).

Of course, there are parental inequities in all families. And in all families, these inequities are often the cause of some distress. However, the inequities that arise in families of children with autism are often far more substantial, extensive, and consistent than those in other families. For example, children with autism may frequently get new toys to keep them motivated or may be allowed to eat snacks even when it is close to dinner if they are working on a skill. They may also get more of their parents' attention, because their behaviors and characteristics demand more attention in an ongoing manner.

It is a good idea to address unequal treatment, or even perceptions of unequal treatment, with your other children, since it may negatively affect the relationship between siblings. Suggestions include:

1. Try to minimize unequal treatment to the extent possible. (For example, when your other children are quite young, give them small rewards for mastering new skills too.) Consider putting everyone on a reinforcement system for good behavior. Also try to ensure that each of your children gets some special time alone with you.
2. Explain to your other children why their sibling with autism requires differential treatment. For example, you might tell your preschool-aged child that her brother has not yet learned to talk and is having trouble learning. An older child may be able to understand that autism is a problem in the brain that affects learning and behavior.
3. Pay attention to your other children's feelings about what they may see as preferential treatment. If they do have concerns about fairness, solicit specific input on what seems unfair *and* on what would make them feel more fairly treated.
4. Make sure they know how very proud you are of them for their accomplishments. Show interest in their activities. Make time to discuss their challenges or struggles. Be involved in their schoolwork, even if they do not need assistance. Spend time reviewing their projects, reports, and homework.

It is also important to bear in mind that there are other stresses such as grandparent illness, job loss, or financial difficulties that can have an impact on your children (Macks & Reeve, 2007; Orsmond & Seltzer, 2009). In fact, the addition of other stresses on top of the stress of having a brother or sister with autism can place siblings at greater risk for experiencing the negative effects of stress. If you can reduce other sources of stress, it may have positive (though indirect) benefits on helping your other children cope with family life.

When More Than One Child Has Autism

Some families have more than one child on the autism spectrum. In some cases, younger siblings have been watched carefully because of an older sibling's diagnosis of autism. Often, these children are identified early and have access to services at very young ages. This is a positive change that has resulted from increased awareness of the autism spectrum and better early diagnostic tools. On the negative side, however, it can take an emotional toll on parents to monitor their children's development so vigilantly.

If more than one child is diagnosed with autism, families must cope with the distinct and significant needs of more than one child with developmental challenges. This can definitely increase parental stress and worry, as well as the challenges of coping.

From a sibling perspective, having more than one child with autism in the family has several effects. If there are nondisabled siblings as well, they will need to cope with special attention being given to more than one brother or sister. Generally, this will make it even more challenging for them to get parental attention, and it may highlight some of the inequity issues covered above. In these cases, it is very important for the typically developing sibling to get his or her needs met. These needs may include:

- time away from caretaking (i.e., time when they can be just a kid, rather than always helping care for, or teach, their siblings with autism),
- respite from the siblings with autism,
- dedicated time from parents for just him or her, and
- introduction to a community of other siblings with similar experiences.

If all of the siblings have autism, it is likely that there are varying degrees. That can be challenging for any of them. The children who have more skills or abilities may not see themselves as similar to their more affected sibling(s). Children who are more affected may be aware that their brother or sister can do things that they can't do. Parents must make a special effort to not group their children with autism together because of a shared disability, but to continue to treat each as an individual. The burden on parents in this scenario is enormous, although many manage this with grace and success.

What We Can Learn from Adult Siblings

Siblings of children with autism journey through life with their brother or sister. We can learn a great deal from their retrospective reflections on the experience of growing up with a sibling on the spectrum. In-depth interviews with many of these siblings (Feiges & Weiss, 2004) focus us on both the challenges and the benefits associated with the role.

Some of the themes convey some struggles (e.g., in balancing caretaking with the need for independence), but there are also clearly many benefits associated with the role. Many adults who grew up with siblings on the autism spectrum are committed to improving the lives of those less fortunate, are tolerant and understanding of others who have special needs, and see the experience as broadening and deepening their humanity.

Following are some insights about growing up with a brother or sister with autism that were shared by adult siblings:

Role definition:

- *"One thing I struggle with today is that I feel more like a mother than I do a sister. I think my relationship with Rick is very complex because I feel like a mother, sister, therapist, friend, nurse. That becomes extremely emotional. I am always helping him with something."*

Tendency to be a caretaker:

- *"I am usually the caretaker in personal relationships. Whenever I am with my friends, I tend to be the one talking about responsibility and the one who's there to listen and help with my friend's problems."*

Sense of mission/helping professions:

- *"What it has given me is that I can listen to clients (as a social worker) for hours and hours because I'm used to waiting! I'm patient and interested. When I got my master's in social work, a friend commented to me that when I was born, they didn't say, 'It's a girl,' they said, 'It's a social worker!' I was born to heal and do family therapy."*

- *"My parents have taught me incredible values about taking care of people, and whether it is Joseph or a homeless man—there's this ethical value that it is our obligation and also our honor to take care of the downtrodden. Because of this, I have been given the wonderful profession of therapist that comes totally naturally and makes me feel that I have a purpose in life. It has made me a better person to be forced to see someone else's needs first."*

Strengthening of the family and appreciation of the sibling:

- *"Chris has brought us closer in a way you can't describe. He's the focus of our family, basically, in terms of how we think. He's the glue and he's shaped how my sister and I think and act."*

- *"Todd contributes so much to the family. . . . His best characteristic is his personality. He is almost always smiling or laughing. . . . I love Todd very much and my relationship with him is one of, if not the most, cherished relationship in my life."*

Compassion and tolerance:

- *"I am a much more patient person than most of my friends. Also, I am not as prejudiced and a lot more open-minded."*

- *"Chris has given me a broader perspective. I can relate to different people and he has taught me to be more accepting."*

Summary

Siblings of children with autism are faced with a unique and significant set of challenges. It is important to support siblings, to help them solve problems creatively, and to provide them with concrete skills for successful interactions with their brother or sister. Parents and clinicians should ensure that they provide support and training that is matched to the child's developmental level. Furthermore, parents should encourage siblings to express their feelings, both positive and negative, about living with a brother or sister with autism.

What is the bottom line regarding sibling experience? Siblings of children with autism often do experience powerful negative emotions from time to time. However, they will also often feel later in life that being a sibling of a person with autism has made them strong, compassionate, and tolerant. No one chooses to become a sibling of a person with an autism spectrum disorder, but many siblings report finding hope, meaning, and happiness through this accidental role.

References

Celiberti, D.A. & Harris, S.L. (1993). Behavioral intervention for siblings of children with autism: A focus on skills to enhance play. *Behavior Therapy 24,* 573-99.

Feiges, L. S. & Weiss, M. J (2004). *Sibling stories: Growing Up with a Brother or Sister on the Autism Spectrum.* Shawnee Mission, KS: Autism Asperger Publishing Company.

Harris, S. L. & Glasberg, B. (2003). *Siblings of Children with Autism: A guide for Families.* 2nd ed. Bethesda, MD: Woodbine House.

Hastings, R. P. (2003). Behavioral adjustment of siblings of children with autism. *Journal of Autism and Developmental Disorders 33,* 99-104.

Hastings, R. P. (2007). Longitudinal relationships between sibling behavioral adjustment and behavior problems of children with developmental disabilities. *Journal of Autism and Developmental Disorders 37,* 1485-1492.

Kaminsky, L. & Dewey, D. (2002). Psychosocial adjustment in siblings of children with autism. *Journal of Child Psychology and Psychiatry 43,* 2235-232.

Macks, R. J. & Reeve, R. (2007). The adjustment of non-disabled siblings of children with autism. *Journal of Autism and Developmental Disorders 37,* 1060-1067.

McHale, S. M. & Gamble, W. C. (1989). Sibling relationships and adjustment of children with disabled brothers and sisters. *Journal of Children in Contemporary Society 19,* 131-58.

McHale, S. M. & Pawletko, T. M. (1992). Differential treatment of siblings in two family contexts. *Child Development 63,* 68-81.

McHale, S. M., Updegraff, K.A., Jackson-Newman, J., Tucker, C. J. & Crouter, A. C. (2000). When does parents' differential treatment have negative implications for siblings? *Social Development 9,* 149-72.

Orsmond, G. I. & Seltzer, M. M. (2009). Adolescent siblings of individuals with an autism spectrum disorder: Testing a diathesis-stress model of sibling well-being. *Journal of Autism and Developmental Disorders 39*, 1053-1065.

Rivers, J. W. & Stoneman, Z. (2008). Child temperaments, differential parenting, and the sibling relationships of children with autism spectrum disorders. *Journal of Autism and Developmental Disorders 38*, 1740-1750

Index

Page numbers with a *t* indicate tables.

About the Authors

Mary Jane Weiss, Ph.D., BCBA-D is a Professor at Endicott College, where she directs the Master's Program in ABA and Autism. She previously served as Director of Research and Training and as Clinical Director of the Douglass Developmental Disabilities Center at Rutgers University for 16 years. Her clinical and research interests center on defining best practice ABA techniques, on evaluating the impact of ABA in learners with autism, and in maximizing family members' expertise and adaptation.

Valbona Demiri, Ph.D., BCBA-D is Clinical Director at Reach for the Stars Learning Center in Brooklyn, NY. She was formerly an assistant director of Outreach Services at the Douglass Developmental Disabilities Center, where she clinically oversaw the Early Intervention program. Her professional interests include diagnostic assessments, language and social skills development in very young children, as well as international training of Applied Behavior Analysis. She is a frequent presenter at local and national conferences.